THE LAWYER'S EDITING MANUAL

THE LAWYER'S EDITING MANUAL

Joan Ames Magat

CAROLINA ACADEMIC PRESS

Durham, North Carolina

Library of Congress Cataloging-in-Publication Data

Magat, Joan Ames.
  The lawyer's editing manual / Joan Ames Magat. — 1st ed.
      p. cm.
  Includes index.
  ISBN 978-1-59460-538-3 (alk. paper)
  1. Legal composition. 2. Editing. I. Title.
  KF250.M24 2008
  808'.06634—dc22   2008035210

Carolina Academic Press
700 Kent Street
Durham, NC 27701
Phone (919) 489-7486
Fax (919) 493-5668
www.cap-press.com

Printed in the United States of America

Dedicated to the memory of Wes, who was more to me than I can ever say, and to our daughters, whose flesh, bones, and spirits express the depth of his goodness, his intelligence, and his love.

Contents

Foreword

Whazzit?

This manual began as a defensive maneuver: as the faculty editor of a law journal, I am sensitive to authors' published grumbles that student editors don't know enough about effective writing to be up to their task. So the manual was initially a compendium of rules and conventions that would be useful to student editors seeking guidance or support for their editorial impulses. It is that, still. But it soon became apparent that the manual would be of use to a much broader audience: lawyers, law clerks, and law students (including those editing journals) — anyone involved in drafting, polishing, or editing formal legal documents, from client letters to memoranda and briefs, to scholarly articles, to judicial opinions. For these, this manual should be a nifty but reasonably comprehensive tool as handy and indispensable as *The Bluebook*, focused not on citations but on text.

What are called "rules" here are sometimes disputable, "conventions" even more so. The only reason to be sticklers about using these consistently is to ease the reader's way: writing well (and editing to make writing better) is, after all, about *the reader*. The choice and order of words and their punctuation are simply signals that trigger reader comprehension; their arrangement on the page can facilitate or impede that comprehension, can make the reading a pleasure or a drudge.

An aside about sexist pronouns: The fracas over how to avoid favoritism has gone on for some time, and, apart from such efficient (and perhaps ephemeral) unisex inventions as s/he or the constraining cop-out of using only plurals, it appears to remain unresolved. How to deal with the issue is, to my mind, a matter of taste; our choice of pronouns is not what enslaves women or keeps men oblivious to the offense of the omnipresent "he." One currently popular convention is to vary the sex of the personage, signaling to the reader that it simply doesn't matter whether he reads or she writes or vice versa; what matters is what's read and what's written, and how. That convention is as good as any other and is thus what I use here.

Sources

For the manual's rules and conventions, I consulted such respected sources as *The Chicago Manual of Style* (15th ed.); H.W. Fowler, *A Dictionary of Modern English Usage* (2d ed. 1965); *Webster's Dictionary of English Usage* (1989); *A Dictionary of Modern Legal Usage* (1995) and *The Redbook*, both by Bryan Garner; the *Texas Law Review Manual on Usage, Style & Editing* (9th ed.); William Strunk Jr. and E.B. White, *The Elements of Style* (4th ed. 2000); and Frederick Crews, *The Random House Handbook* (1974); among multiple others, including, of course,

Webster's Collegiate Dictionary (11th ed.), *Black's Law Dictionary* (8th ed.), and *The Bluebook* (18th ed.). *Bluebook* rules are cited and, in some instances, quoted for convenience' sake. Consulting a multiplicity of the sources, I figured, would support treating as rules what is really just conventional practice (because our language, as a tool for our times, is ever in flux). Predictably, though, not all rules and conventions are supported by consensus. This manual does not enter the debate, but it does support its choices with explanation. It is easier for the writer or editor not just to defend, but to remember a convention when the logic of the choice is expressed, as well.

The Examples

Some passages illustrating these rules and conventions I dreamed up; others I borrowed from recent law-review articles and, occasionally, judicial opinions. Authorship of passages not modified beyond recognition is acknowledged in Endnotes. To avoid distracting the reader unnecessarily, quotation marks are not used to signal original language, though modification is indicated with brackets and ellipses. An exception is section III on QUOTATIONS, where indicating quotation marks is indispensable. The sources supporting certain conventions about which reasonable minds may differ are annotated likewise. And reasonable minds do differ, if for no other reason than that our language is evolving.

A Word about Legal Prose Style

The style of legal writing—whether it be academic, judicial, or professional—is formal and, to some extent, technical, in that its patterns tend to be somewhat rigid and predictable. The reason for the rigidity and formality is surely to present the document's content to the busy reader—the judge, the partner or associate—in a predictable medium that is easily negotiated and that does not itself distract from the message. More and more academic authors, however, write in the style of articulate, serious, documented journalism, which is more colloquial in tone. The only rule that might be said to apply to legal style overall, whatever form it takes, is that it ease and not inhibit the reader's comprehension—that it be correct, clear, and consistent. Otherwise, the author is entitled to great leeway. This manual includes a section on Usage and Style that might sensitize the writer and editor to what makes one passage sing and another one grate. It is not—and cannot be—comprehensive. My intention here is to prompt the editorial ear to hear and distinguish between the music and the noise, whether that be in the writing one is editing or in the editor's own prose.

A Word for the Student Editor: The Limits of Editorial Interference

The legal writer in general and the student editor in particular should be ruthless in scrutinizing her own writing for incorrectness or ineffectiveness and in revising, revising, revising to make her prose pellucid. Her dealings with the writing of others, however, should be restrained by considerable tact. Authors will accept an edit that *corrects error* without cavil; but most academic authors are sufficiently confident of their writing skills that suggested edits for *effectiveness* may well offend unless carefully proffered.

In short, edits to prose should first follow identifiable principles such as those described in this manual. An editor should never suggest changing text to something that "sounds better" to her, regardless of how well-attuned her ear, without knowing *why* it sounds better. Then, the *why* behind such optional edits should be explained in a comment bubble or another unintrusive but clearly delineated text.

How to Use This Manual

Rules of Thumb & Pencils

Because reasonable minds may (and will) differ about what writing practices are "right" and "wrong" (and because this is certainly so in an increasingly global legal world), this manual does not pretend to present definitive rules. But it does offer rules of thumb—common-practice answers for questions that typically arise regarding legal prose. Whether a practice is, in fact, "common" is doubtless contestable. But all these conventions, these rules of thumb, rest on this premise: Writing is for the reader. It follows that writing conventions should be consistent so as not to distract the reader or confound his expectations, and that such conventions should facilitate the read.

Nonetheless, this manual comes with a virtual pencil. For despite the logic and common practices underlying the rules of thumb listed and illustrated here, different practices might be preferred; if they are, they should be noted so that whatever practice is preferred, it is consistently followed.

Terminology

American law students have typically heard, read, and written enough correct English to have developed an ear for correct language patterns; so they typically have little use for the labels used by grammarians and linguists to describe the rules and conventions that govern clear and effective writing. If students once knew the names of these patterns, they may well have forgotten them by now. But when we need to communicate about these rules and conventions, the labels come in handy. So this manual uses such labels to describe a language pattern or to refer to one. They are defined in the glossary at the end, which also indexes their use.

Organization & Layout:

This manual is organized into five substantive sections: I. GRAMMAR, II. PUNCTUATION, III. QUOTATIONS, IV. USAGE & STYLE, and V. CONVENTIONS. To some extent, the order signifies assumptions about use: from the first section to the last, the rules (such as they are) stated and illustrated track a kind of progression from practices that should be followed consistently because they are widely viewed as "correct" (grammar, punctuation) to practices that should be followed consistently (usage, style, conventions) because they enable the efficient (and enjoyable) read.

GRAMMAR comes first because its rules are the most definite, the least debatable. This section introduces the terminology that the remainder of the manual uses, it lists grammatical errors that occur most often, and it dispels myths about presumptive grammatical errors that are not, in fact, wrong. PUNCTUATION is next because its rules, like those governing grammar, follow a logic that tends to remain relatively constant. This is followed by an important section on introducing and using QUOTATIONS. The section on USAGE & STYLE includes entries on not only effective word choice but effective sentence and paragraph structure; the CONVENTIONS section offers options about capitalization, the use of italics, spelling, and so forth. Some of these track and reference *Bluebook* rules; others track and reference conventions suggested in the *Chicago Manual of Style*.

Rules and conventions are stated in the left-hand column of each page. Examples of their application are given in the column on the right.

Subject
(and definition or description when considered necessary)

Sub-subject
(and definition or description when considered necessary)

Rule or convention stated and explained in this column	**Examples** shown in this column
	comments
comments	

Many rules are illustrated with a simple (if not simplistic) example. Some are accompanied as well by a sentence quoted or paraphrased from a published law-review article—for what may appear obvious when illustrated briefly and plainly can be harder to see in the real world of more complex text. When necessary, the example or the rule or convention itself is accompanied by comments in italics.

Approaching the Contents

The quickest way to find a rule on a particular subject—say, commas—is via the TABLE OF CONTENTS. If an editor cannot recall what a serial comma is, for example, the GLOSSARY & INDEX is the better approach. Or an editor might find it helpful to simply peruse a particular section—such as I. GRAMMAR: Verbs: Tenses—to review, for example, when to use past progressive versus the past tense.

Acknowledgments

Thanks, first, to those who encouraged me to pursue this project, including most prominently my loving daughters, Marin and Claire.

Thanks, next, to its earliest proofreaders, Claire and Marin, again, and Ian Houseal, for spending more than one summer day sunk in the task and for offering many a practical and clarifying suggestion.

Thanks, then, to the line of editors-in-chief of *Law & Contemporary Problems*, from Chris Hart (2004–2005), who thought that such a little book would come in handy for law students editing law-review text, to Anne Hazlett (2006–2007), Sarah Hawkins (2007–2008), and Jeff Mason (2008–2009) who readily adopted the manual, in its rough early versions, for use by their own editorial staffs. And thanks to the members of those staffs, whose reliance on the manual's conventions and whose suggestions for modifications and amendments strengthened both the manual and the consistency and quality of their own editing.

And thanks to the later proofreaders—Sarah, again, who reviewed and approved new sections and, most notably, Anne Beaumont, who devoted at least one transcontinental flight to its scrutiny and who caught and corrected many, many errors and obscurities that had eluded me. That Anne had been an editor before she came to Duke Law School was too fortuitous for me not to exploit. She knows the depth of my appreciation; but I still owe her.

Finally, thanks to my students in the Advanced Legal Writing Workshop, whose use of the manual lent a common vocabulary to principled, comprehensible suggestions for revision in their peer reviews of their classmates' work. (Such effective editing, though, would have been impossible without the students' having exercised their own astuteness, intelligence, and kindness in the peer-reviewing task.)

And thanks to Keith Sipe and Tim Colton and the rest of the crew at Carolina Academic Press, for seeing the usefulness of this manual not only for law-review editors, but for lawyers in practice. Thanks to them, too, of course, for bringing it to fruition.

Abbreviations

NB   *nota bene*, note well

Cf.   compare

a.k.a.   also known as

→   this arrow is intended simply to direct the reader's eye to something that follows—usually, the revision of the passage given in any one example

≠   is not the same as

WEBSTER'S
     Webster's Collegiate Dictionary (11th ed.),

BLACK'S
     Black's Law Dictionary (8th ed.)

CHICAGO MANUAL
     The Chicago Manual of Style (15th ed.)

FOWLER, MODERN ENGLISH USAGE
     H.W. Fowler, *A Dictionary of Modern English Usage* (2d ed. 1965)

GARNER, MODERN LEGAL USAGE
     Brian A. Garner, *A Dictionary of Modern Legal Usage* (2d ed. 1995)

BLUEBOOK
     The Bluebook (18th ed.)

THE LAWYER'S EDITING MANUAL

I

Grammar: What's What

This section addresses whether sentences are put together *correctly* — that is, in ways that most educated readers expect to see and thus most readily comprehend. Writers take liberties in the name of style, but formal prose should generally abide by rules that the following sections define and address.

Verbs

Transitive Verbs & Intransitive Verbs:
Which is which (a)–(c), and so what (d)–(f)?

Many usage questions can be resolved by knowing whether a verb is transitive or intransitive or both.

(a) Transitive verbs need a direct object. (It did *what*.)	***To lay** (meaning to put) **is transitive:*** **Lay** *the hay* on the haystack. You **laid** *the hay* on the haystack yesterday. You **have laid** *the hay* on the haystack day after day.
(b) Intransitive verbs do not need a direct object. (It simply did.)	***To lie** (meaning to be prostrate) **is intransitive:*** **Lie** on the haystack. You **lay** on the haystack all day yesterday. You **have lain** on the haystack every afternoon since summer began.
(c) Many verbs are both transitive and intransitive. Check the dictionary: evolve … \ *vb* **evolved; evolv•ing** [L *evolvere* to unroll, fr. *e-* + *volvere* to roll … *vt* (1775) **1 :** EMIT **2a :** DERIVE, EDUCE **b :** to produce by natural evolutionary processes **c :** develop, work out <~social, political, and literary philosophies -L. W. Doob> ~ *vi* : to undergo evolutionary change— … WEBSTER'S	The Galapagos finches evolved a wide variation of beak size and shape. *(evolved what? = transitive)* Variation in beak size and shape evolved. *(evolved, period = intransitive)*

(d) Transitive verbs need no preposition.	consult (*vt*): She consulted her editor.
(e) Intransitive verbs cannot take an object without a preposition.	confer (*vi*): She conferred **with** her editor.
(f) A transitive verb can be passive; an intransitive verb cannot.	She was consulted by her editor.

Verb Tenses

Verb tenses indicate actions along a time line.

Before Yesterday	Yesterday	Today	Tomorrow
Past Perfect	(Simple) Past	Present	Future

A verb's tense indicates when the action takes place: past (e.g., yesterday), present (now), and future (e.g., tomorrow).	**Present:** The defendant **pleads** not guilty. *It is or happens now or in general.* **(Simple) Past:** The defendant **pled (or pleaded)** not guilty. *It happened; it's over.* **Future:** The defendant **will plead** not guilty. *It's going to happen. Needs an "auxiliary" verb.*

When writing about law, use past (or past perfect) to discuss events that have taken place; use present tense to discuss the law itself, so long as it is viable.

Example:
Title VII prohibits [present] discrimination in the workplace based on unequal pay for men and women performing the same work. But **the Court held** [past] in *Ledbetter v. Goodyear Tire and Rubber Co.* that the plaintiff, **who had filed** [past perfect] a complaint with the EEOC more than 180 days after the first instance of that discrimination, **was** [past] time-barred from seeking relief under that law.

Similarly, present tense can be used in writing about writing: that the author wrote it is past; it's over with. But what is written, like the law, in a sense lives on and can (but need not) be described in the present tense.

Example:

Justice Alito, writing for the majority in *Ledbetter,* **makes** rare but effective use of the emphatic one-sentence paragraph. After quoting Justice Stevens' remark in *United Airlines, Inc. v. Evans*, 431 U.S. 553 (1977), that a discriminatory act not followed by a timely charge is merely an "unfortunate event [without] legal consequences," *id.* at 558, Alito **concludes,** "It would be difficult to speak to the point more directly." *Ledbetter,* 127 S. Ct. 2162, 2168 (2007).

The "perfect" forms of these tenses indicate an action preceding another. They are formed with an auxiliary verb (is, has) in the past, present, or future tense, plus the past participle for the action.

Participles: When used with an auxiliary verb (is, has, do), past participles indicate action in the past; present participles indicate action in the present or future. Some past participles have more than one form (has **pled**, has **pleaded**).

Present perfect: auxiliary + past participle
The defendant **has pled** (or **has pleaded**) not guilty.
> *It happened before now, but it is current; that is, it just happened.*

Past perfect: past auxiliary + past participle
Before the defendant pled guilty yesterday, he **had pled** (or **had pleaded**) not guilty four times.
> *It happened before the simple past.*

Future Perfect: future auxiliary + past participle
The defendant **will have** (**shall have**) **pled** (or **will have** (**shall have**) **pleaded**) not guilty for the fourth time.
> *For use of "shall," see* IV. USAGE & STYLE: Auxiliary Verbs.

The "progressive" forms of these tenses indicate an action that is ongoing.

Present progressive: is + present participle
Right now, the defendant is pleading not guilty.

Past progressive: was + present participle
Until today, the defendant was pleading not guilty.

Future progressive: will be / shall be + present participle
Later, the defendant will be/shall be pleading guilty.

Present perfect progressive: has been + present participle
The defendant has been pleading not guilty since time immemorial.

Past perfect progressive: had been + present participle
The defendant had been pleading not guilty when he suddenly recalled he was probably otherwise.

Future perfect progressive: will have been + past participle
By the time he is finally tried, the defendant will have been pleading not guilty for six months.

Verbs: Mood

Unlike tenses, which indicate time, mood indicates the writer's attitude about the subject. The **indicative** states or asks what is, the **subjunctive** most often expresses conditional circumstances, and the **imperative** commands.

For **person** (e.g., first v. third) and **voice** (e.g., passive v. active), see IV. USAGE & STYLE.

Indicative mood: statement, question	• The foreman **rises** when he announces the verdict. • He did not hurry, so **he is** late. • Each juror **votes** when so bid by the foreman.

Subjunctive mood: when used

See also I. GRAMMAR: Subjunctive Mood — How to Form, below. *See also* IV. USAGE & STYLE: Auxiliary Verbs.

(a) conditional: expresses a condition (e.g., hypothetical) or wish or probability (or improbability, possibility, or situation contrary to fact) **(i)** often after *if, as if, suppose,* etc.) or **(ii)** accompanied by an auxiliary expressing a condition — *may, might, could, should,* or *would*	**(i)** If only this decision **were** overturned! **(ii) Should** this decision **be** overruled, it **would appall** us all. **(ii)** This protocol **might** simply **increase** the amount of input without assuring any improvement overall.

(b) reportorial: used in clauses that are the direct object of a verb expressing requirements or recommendations — verbs such as *ask, command, recommend, urge, insist, request, suggest, require,* or *move.*
 	
Cf. An alternative construction, which eliminates the need for the relative pronoun *that,* uses the full indicative form of the verb, rather than the subjunctive.
	• The clerk **commands that** the foreman **rise** to announce the verdict.
	  Cf. The clerk commands the foreman **to rise** to announce the verdict.
	• The chair **asked that** everyone present **vote.**
	  Cf. The chair asked everyone present **to vote.**

(c) certain formulaic expressions	• as it were • let it be known • be that as it may • come what may

Subjunctive Mood: How to Form

(a) **for conditional expressing improbability, etc.,** use the verb root (the indicative without the *to*) → ~~to~~ hurry, ~~to~~ be.	• It cannot **be**! • He **be** wrong?! Unimaginable!
(b) **for conditional expressing present hypothetical or wish,**	

(i) **use the past form of the auxiliary verb:**
     is → **were**;
     can → **could**;
     may → **might**;
     shall → **should**;
     will → **would**
	• Suppose he **were** here.
	 • If only he **were** here.

(ii) **for verbs other than these, add the verb root to the auxiliary.**	• If only he **would come**.
(c) **for conditional expressing past hypothetical or wish,** use past perfect.	• Suppose he **had come**. • We **should have known** he could not come. • If only he **had been** here.
(d) **for reportorial use:** that + verb root (the indicative without the *to*) → ~~to~~ pronounce, ~~to~~ be.	• The judge asked **that** the foreman please **pronounce** the jury's verdict. • I insist **that** you **be** still. • The foreman bade **that** each juror **vote**.
Imperative mood: orders, commands, etc.: third person singular	Hear ye!

Verbals

Verbals (infinitives, participles, & gerunds) share the characteristics of a verb with those of a noun.

An infinitive is a verb in the rough, as it were, the verb before tense or mood or person gets to it. It can function **(a)** as part of a verb phrase or **(b)** as a noun.	**(a)** We need **to hurry**. **(b)** **To laugh** is **to live**.
It **may** be split by an adverb if such placement is more effective.	It is better **to heartily laugh** than to heartily cry.

A **gerund**, formed by adding –ing to a verb root, is a **noun**.

- **Holding** a run-off election is the only solution.

If someone is doing it, the action belongs to that someone, who needs a possessive apostrophe (plus "s"). The possessive is not always required, as the "holding" example above illustrates; rather, it is required when it is important to specify who is the agent of the action, as when the subject of the sentence is different from the agent. *See* Fowler, Modern English Usage 225–26.

- Jones won by **Smith's missing** a chance. Fowler, Modern English Usage 225.

In some contexts, the possessive is the only way to distinguish a **gerund** from a **present participle** (see below). So: What's the difference?

- The lady's **holding the broom** was a tipoff that she was a witch.

The apostrophe signaling that the –ing form of the verb is a **gerund** subtly focuses the reader's attention on the action, rather than on the actor. Why? Because a noun (signaled by the possessive apostrophe) is a thing in and of itself — not a mere adjective (a participle) describing another noun.

- The danger was the CEO's **picking and choosing** among the company's commitments.

See also II. PUNCTUATION: Apostrophes.

A **present participle**, formed by adding –ing to a verb root, functions as an **adjective**. Using a participle signals, ever so subtly, that the actor is more important than the action.

- **The lady** [who was] **holding** the broom is a witch.
- The danger was **the CEO** [who was] **picking and choosing** among the company's commitments.

Present participles & explanatory parentheticals: When these begin with present participles, the phrase introduced functions as an **adjective** insofar as it describes the court's action.

- Party v. Party, cite (**holding** …)

- State v. Defendant, cite (**finding** …)

Absolute Phrases

An absolute phrase modifies the whole sentence.

An **absolute phrase** usually precedes the sentence and may appear to modify the subject that immediately follows the phrase, but it does not; rather, it modifies the entire sentence. An absolute phrase is thus not a dangling participle, though it may look like one.	Considering what a fool we thought he was, his riposte struck us as brilliant. *"Considering" is not a participle modifying "his riposte"; the phrase beginning with "Considering" modifies the main clause, "his riposte struck us as brilliant."*
Cf. a participial phrase that modifies the subject in the main clause	**Cf.** Considering his options, he chose to respond with a withering ripost. *"Considering …" here is a participial phrase modifying "he."*

Appositives

An appositive construction is the restatement of a noun or noun phrase that further defines it.

The appositive element (word or phrase) may be set off
    (a) by commas (when relatively short and nondefining)
    or
    (b) by em dashes (which tolerate a longer appositive phrase or one with internal commas).
	(a) The boy, an orphan, had stowed away.
	
	(b) The boy — an orphan who had escaped his kind but overbearing guardians as soon as he could outrun them — had stowed away.

When the appositive element is set off by another word or phrase signaling the appositive nature of the material that follows (*namely, for example, or, that is,* etc.), it is likewise set off with a comma or an em dash.	• The boy was an orphan — namely, one without kin. • The boy was nameless, namely, neither Tom nor Dick nor Harry.
When the appositive phrase is an independent clause, it can be set off with a colon or semicolon.	• The boy was an orphan; that is, he had no kin. • The boy was an orphan; he had no kin. • The boy was an orphan: he had no kin.

Articles

For whether words require an article, see I. GRAMMAR: Which Article? Chart, below.

the versus *a* versus **[no article]**

the, a definite article, indicates a definite or specific object with which the reader is already familiar or one whose familiarity is inherent in the context of the sentence, so further identifying information is unnecessary.	• **The** hat on **the** table is mine. ***Cf.*** Someone left **a** hat on the table.
NB: ***The*** can indicate a class or genre rather than a specific individual.	• You know the type: **the uncaring, self-involved mother.**
a or ***an***, indefinite articles, point to nonspecific or generic objects. ***A*** cannot precede plurals.	• **A** stitch in time saves nine.

a or *an?*

Like any other noun taking an indefinite article, whether *a* or *an* is used depends on whether the initial sound of the noun is pronounced as a consonant or as a vowel.	• an accident of history • a historical accident • an heir apparent • a hair-raising scheme
Vowel sounds (including the letters F, H, L, M, N, R, S, X) take ***an***, consonant sounds take ***a***.	• a ubiquity of law • an S, followed by an F

For whether to use articles with abbreviations, *see* V. CONVENTIONS: Abbreviations — Articles & Acronyms or Initialisms.

Articles & coordinate nouns

(a) Repeat the article for each noun **unless**	• the owl and **the** pussycat • The play explored the effects of rebellion on **the** individual, **the** family, and **the** community.
(b) all nouns share the same article and the writer wishes to emphasize their commonality rather than their separateness.	• The play explored the effects of rebellion on **the** individual, family, and community.
(c) Similarly, using a single article for coordinate nouns can imply that they are a single unit.	• At once **a horse and cart** appeared. • This administration is just **a dog and pony show.**

Coordinate Adjectives, Compound Modifiers, & Compound Nouns

Sometimes it is hard to tell whether an adjective is a single modifier, whether it is part of a **compound modifier,** or whether it is actually part of a **compound noun.** Which is which has consequences for punctuation. *See* II. PUNCTUATION: Commas & Coordinate Adjectives; II. PUNCTUATION: Commas & Coordinate Adjectives, Compound Modifiers, & Compound Nouns. *See also* II. PUNCTUATION: Hyphens.

Grammatical Missteps (or not)

Agreement: subject & verb & number: The number of subject(s) and that indicated by the verb must agree.

(a) Be aware of singular nouns that signify a group — e.g., *majority, government, board*

and of

- A **majority** of the voters typically **rejects** lottery bonds.

(b) singular nouns that, modified with a prepositional phrase, may sound plural, e.g., *each* or *none.*

- **Each** of the voters **intends** to vote.
- **None** of the voters **intends** to vote.

(c) Likewise, the number indicated by the noun and that indicated by its pronoun must agree.

- If **a youth** fails to meet ~~their~~ → his or her obligations, ~~they~~ → he or she can be sent to detention.

(d) When a singular and a plural noun are represented by a single pronoun, the pronoun should agree with the latter noun.

- Snopes's key feature is its "Urban Legend Reference Pages," which **aim** to provide accurate information about rumors on various topics…."[1]

- If the exculpatory DNA samples or **the accuser's history** of mendacity had been discovered earlier, **it** would have saved the accused much grief.

    Cf. If the accuser's history of mendacity or **the exculpatory DNA samples** had been discovered earlier, **they** would have saved the accused much grief.

Ambiguous antecedent: a pronoun that can refer to more than one preceding noun and is thus unclear.

The data reveals an unusual number of adverse reactions to the product. If **it** is not to damage the manufacturer's market, **it** will have to be carefully explained in the advertising.
What does "it" refer to? "Data" or "number"?

Coordinating conjunctions: It is perfectly acceptable to begin a sentence with a **coordinating conjunction**. In fact, these are often effective links between sentences.	But it was not meant to be. Or was it?
Dangling participle: a participial phrase preceding the main clause that appears to refer to something other than the subject it modifies	*Dangling:* Aghast, aware his doom was nigh, the pirate ship evoked his cry. *[Who is aghast? Who is aware? Not the pirate ship.]* *No longer dangling:* Aghast, aware his doom was nigh, the lad lost his nerve and began to cry.
Cf. **Absolute phrase**, which clearly modifies the entire sentence	*Absolute phrase:* **When considering possible crossover of Republicans and Democrats,** the immeasurable number of possible permutations must be kept in mind.

Parallel Structure

Sentence elements that are syntactically parallel should be grammatically parallel. *See also* IV. USAGE & STYLE: Effectiveness & Emphasis — Repetition.

Parallel structure, generally When the sentence structures two or more things or actions as pairs or triplets, etc., their forms should match.	• She was **a brain** as well as **a beauty**. (article + noun — article + noun) • He could not only **sing**, but also **dance** and **play the tambourine** — simultaneously. (verb — verb — verb phrase)
Parallel structure & verb phrases Each verb in a parallel list of verb phrases must have the same grammatical form (i.e., past tense–past tense; participle–participle; infinitive–infinitive).	*Parallel unclear:* The drug trials sought to determine toxicity by **testing** a range of doses and **examine** whether the drugs were effective. *Parallel clear:* • The drug trials **sought** to determine toxicity by testing a range of doses and **examined** whether the drugs were effective.

• The drug trials sought to determine toxicity by **testing** a range of doses and **examining** whether the drugs were effective.

Parallel structure & (optional) repeated elements Although it is not strictly necessary to repeat each element in parallel phrases, doing so usually makes the parallel more clear.	***Less clear:*** The drug trials sought **to determine** toxicity by testing a range of doses and **examine** whether the drugs were effective. ***More clear:*** The drug trials sought **to determine** toxicity by testing a range of doses and **to examine** whether the drugs were effective.

Apart from decisions driven by style (see italicized comments below), **whether and how much of the verb phrase to repeat** depends on the sentence's length and complexity: the farther apart the parallel elements, the more important is the repetition of the entire verb phrase.

The repeated element may be an article,	I own a horse and a cart. *(emphasizes separateness of items)* ***Cf.*** I own a horse and cart. *(emphasizes functional unit)*
a preposition,	The Commission adopts a process that includes participation **by** nongovernmental players as well as **by** elected officials. ***NB:*** *the prepositions need not be the same one for the construction to be parallel:* The administrators responsible for implementing these programs often play a major role, outside **of** and contrary **to** expectations.
an auxiliary verb,	Administrative procedures **must** be attuned to existing institutional patterns and **must** allow for the intercession of parties whose interests are affected.
the *to* of an infinitive phrase,	• [T]he sociology of legal professional formation dominated by national legal training means the project of global administrative law is likely in practice **to include**, in its constructive aspect, efforts to identify, design, and help build transnational and global structures that can fulfill functions at least

somewhat comparable to those administrative law fulfills domestically, and **to reform** domestic administrative law to enable it to deal with the increasingly global character of regulation.[2]

· According to colonial law, the sovereign governed his subjects outside his territory and could, by charter, confer on them exclusive rights **to trade** or **to settle** outside territory that were enforceable at English law.[3] [citation omitted]

The second "to" in this sentence could have been dropped; the author may have chosen to keep it for rhythm and emphasis.

a coordinating conjunction (e.g., because), or	She left **because** she wanted to, **because** she could, and **because** no one wished her to stay.
a relative pronoun.	An example is this regulatory body, **which** began as a nongovernmental organization, but **which** now includes governmental officials from a number of jurisdictions.
Split infinitive It is permissible to split an infinitive (to + verb root) with a modifier when doing so places it closer to the word modified. Splitting with more than one modifier, though, can be unwieldy.	*Effective & permissible:* The court proceeded **to thoroughly analyze** the merits of disallowing interstate wine sales. *Unwieldy:* The court proceeded **to thoroughly and unambiguously explain** the merits of disallowing interstate wine sales. *Infinitive intact, unwieldiness avoided:* The court proceeded **to explain — thoroughly and unambiguously —** the merits of disallowing interstate wine sales.

Split verb phrase

Verb phrases other than infinitives may be split if putting the modifier right before or right after the key word or phrase modified is effective (as for emphasis) and does not invite ambiguity.

See also IV. USAGE & STYLE: Effective Modifier Placement.

[T]he sovereign governed his subjects outside his territory and could, by charter, confer on them exclusive rights....

Above, the placement of "by charter" modifies and emphasizes the conferring of the rights.

Below, "by charter" is more muffled.

Cf. [T]he sovereign governed his subjects outside his territory and could ... confer on them by charter exclusive rights....[4]

Grammar Charts

Coordinating Conjunctions	Correlative Conjunctions: Don't use one without the other
and or nor but for (meaning because) yet	both ... and either ... or neither ... nor not only ... but [also] **Except:** on the one hand ... on the other hand— (either may be used without the other).

Some Common Conjunctive Adverbs		Subordinating Conjunctions		Relative Pronouns
accordingly	meanwhile	after	now that	that
again	moreover	although	once	what
also	namely	as	provided [that]	whatever
anyway	nevertheless	as far as	since	which
besides	next	as soon as	so that	whichever
consequently	nonetheless	as if	supposing [that]	who
finally	now	as though	than	whoever
further	otherwise	because	that	whosoever
furthermore	rather	before	though	whom
hence	so	even if	till	whomever
however	still	even though	unless	whomsoever
incidentally	that is	however	until	whose
indeed	then	if	when	
instead	therefore	inasmuch as	whenever	
likewise	thus	in case	where	
		in order that	wherever	
		insofar as	whether	
		in that	while	
		lest	why	

Auxiliary Verbs					
is	can	might	need	shall	would
has	may	must	ought	should	

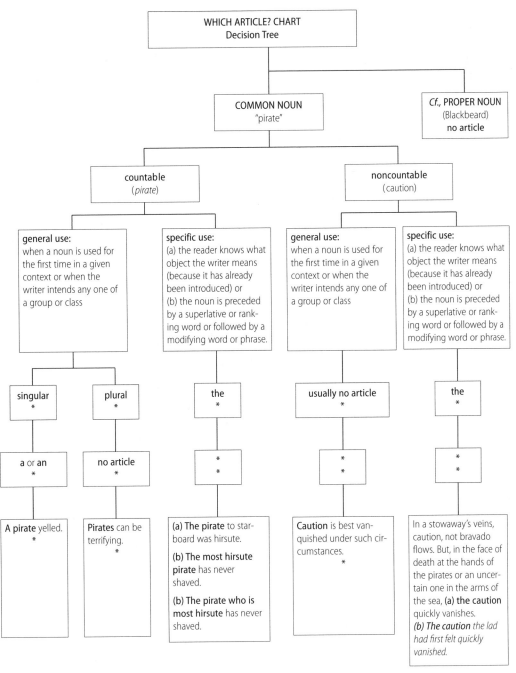

Decision tree adapted from Anne Enquist & Laurel Currie Oates, *Just Writing* 294 (2d ed. 2005).

The question whether to use an article may arise with words that can be both count and noncount nouns and that can be used generally or specifically. For example, *law, evidence.*

countable, general	countable, specific	noncountable, general	noncountable, specific
A law prohibiting smoking in bars has gone into effect. **Laws** prohibiting smoking in bars are ubiquitous.	**The law** prohibiting smoking in bars has gone into effect. **The laws** prohibiting smoking have driven smokers of many nations outside.	I study **law**.	Criminals respect only **the law** of averages.
		Absent **evidence**, crimes are hard to prove.	The **evidence** was damning.

The specific or general use of a noncountable noun drives the decision whether it gets "the." "Criminal law," for instance, is usually referred to as a general use of a noncountable noun. One who wishes to denote its specificity as a field of practice or jurisprudence, though, might append "the."

For articles with abbreviations, see V. CONVENTIONS: Abbreviations — Articles & Acronyms or Initialisms.

II

Punctuation

How It Sounds

Apart from the correctness of their use and the meanings they signify for the content of a sentence, periods, colons, semicolons, commas, em dashes, and parentheses all signal pauses. These pauses vary in length, affecting the rhythm of the sentence.

The **period** is the most definitive pause because it ends the expression of a thought in that sentence.	The boy stood on the burning deck. (full stop) Smoke like a noose slid round his neck. (full stop)
The **colon** also signals a definitive stop, but it promises that the clause or series that will follow continues the thought expressed in the first clause.	The boy stood on the burning deck: he felt its heat from toes to neck.
The **semicolon** is a hybrid of colon and comma: it signals a complete thought that suggests or is further explained by the clause that follows. The length of the pause is about the same as that after a colon. ***Cf.*** em dash (longer).	Flames licked at his ankles; smoke hooded his head; he saw nothing to port; he turned starboard with dread.
The **comma** signals a break long enough to keep two elements in a sentence apart — to preclude ambiguity, to de-emphasize the element set off, or, differently used, to give it emphasis.	• Standing on the burning boards, he starboard spied the pirate hoards.
Parenthetical material enclosed in commas is more closely related to the rest of the sentence than material enclosed in em-dashes or parentheses would be.	• Standing on the burning planks, which, smold'ring, steamed effluvium dank, he felt the heat assault his toes, which, like the smoke, displeased his nose.

The **em dash** sets off parenthetical elements more emphatically than do commas or parentheses. It signals a longer pause than that signaled by a comma.	Standing on the burning boards—off to starboard, pirate hoards—he vanquished caution, fear expunged, and off to port he promptly plunged.
Words or phrases set off in **parentheses** are essentially *whispered*.	Now he wished (too late to pray) that home (in England) he had stayed.

Periods

A **period** signals the end of a grammatically complete sentence.	The boy stood.#The deck burned.
The typographic habit of two spaces after a period or colon has recently and nearly universally been modified to **a single space.**	
(a) A **period** follows each element in most **abbreviations**, but only one marks the end of the sentence.	**(a)** Up in smoke went his hopes that one day he would be both an M.D. and (of course) a J.D.
(b) Do not use periods for **(i)** abbreviations of three letters or more, **(ii)** two-letter abbreviations of international federations, or **(iii)** for entities commonly known by their initials.	**(b)** **(i)** So did expectations to join the AARP. **(ii)** UN, EU **(iii)** The swim teams use the Y pool.
See also V. CONVENTIONS: Abbreviations.	

Periods & ellipses: *See* II. PUNCTUATION: Quotations.

Colons

The **colon** signals the **delivery of specifics** promised in the first clause. The colon says, *here's how* or *why, to wit,* or *the following*.	The horizon was gone: smoke had swallowed the sea.

A colon can connect two independent clauses, the second of which completes the first, as if the colon said, "and this is how."	• [D]omestic regulatory agencies act as part of the global administrative space: they decide issues of foreign or global concern.[1] • National environmental regulators concerned with … greenhouse gas emissions are today often part of a global administration, as well as a purely national one: they are responsible for implementing international environmental law to achieve common objectives....[2]

A colon can follow an independent clause to formally introduce

(a) one or more words (such as a list) or phrases	**(a)** • The pirates' curses were dramatical: baritone and ungrammatical. • [M]utual recognition is a norm that pervades international relations, starting with the basic prerequisite of relations between states: their mutual recognition qua states within a system in which, at least theoretically, such recognition implies privileges and obligations.[3]
or	
(b) one or more independent clauses (statements or questions). **NB:** in this use, each sentence introduced begins with a capital letter. *See also* II. PUNCTUATION: Colons & Capitalization, below.	**(b)** • To gain such an understanding, we ask a series of analytical questions: Why is rulemaking authority implicitly granted or explicitly delegated to an international or transnational body? What are the consequences of such a delegation of authority for the domestic and international distribution of power and resources? Why do some actors rather than others supply such governance?[4]

Colons & Capitalization

Ordinarily, the first letter of an independent clause following the colon is *not* capitalized (unless it begins with a proper noun).	Doom was evidently nigh: the flames at his ankles grew uncomfortably high; the smoke and the soot drew a hood round his head; seeing nothing to port, he turned starboard with dread.

Capitalize the first letter of the first word of an independent clause following the colon when it is formally introduced by the first clause, as if the colon were saying, "and that is this," **and** when the sentence preceding the colon, though **grammatically complete**, is **substantively incomplete** standing on its own.	• Here's what he saw off starboard side: A skull and crossbones rode the tide! • This question leads to another: To whom is the vice president ultimately accountable? • The first and most obvious factor has to do with the basic question a decisionmaker asks when entering a mutual recognition agreement: Can my country live with this degree of extraterritorial law emanating from this or these *specific* actors?[5] • Consider the following example: Income taxes in Germany are based primarily on externally reported accounting profit, so there are strong legal and economic pressures to report income and asset values conservatively.[6]
Capitalize the first letter of the first word of an independent clause following the colon when the clause is the first of more than one introduced sentence or question.	• The boy looked young: His frame was spare. His chin was weak and free of hair. No Adam's apple marked his throat. His voice sang best the treble notes.
Capitalize the first letter of the first word of an independent clause following the colon when it is a direct quotation (bracket capital if quotation begins elsewhere). *See* III. QUOTATIONS.	• The pirates' threats soon reached his ears: "Beware, ye worms, of buccaneers!"

Colons & Other Punctuation

Words, phrases, and clauses following the colon are ordinarily **separated by commas, even if dashes or parentheses are also involved.**	• Doom was evidently nigh: the flames at his ankles grew uncomfortably high, the smoke and the soot drew a hood round his head, and help there was none—he was giddy with dread. • These international standard-setting bodies are particularly relevant to the sectors covered by the transatlantic mutual recognition agreements: the International Standards Organization (ISO) (for a

broad range of standards), the International Electrotechnical Commission (IEC) (for testing and certification standards, Codex Alimentarius (for food-related standards), the International Conference on Harmonization (for pharmaceutical standards)....[7]

Separate the items following the colon with semicolons only if

(a) they are independent clauses not joined by a coordinating conjunction

or

(b) at least one of the phrases has one or more **internal commas**.

(a) Doom was evidently nigh: the flames at his ankles grew uncomfortably high; the smoke and the soot drew a hood round his head; he saw nothing to port so turned starboard with dread.

(b) These international standard-setting bodies are particularly relevant to the sectors covered by the transatlantic mutual recognition agreements: the International Standards Organization (ISO), for a broad range of standards; the International Electrotechnical Commission (IEC), for testing and certification standards; Codex Alimentarius, for food-related standards....[8]

NB: Regardless of whether what follows the colon is a list or words or a phrase or an independent clause, **the clause preceding the colon must be an independent clause**.

This rule can be satisfied with "the following" or "as follows." But why waste words? The sentence can almost always be more interestingly structured.

Not:
In the abstract, the package at its fullest may include: the right to a hearing before a decision is made, the right to have the decision made in an unbiased and impartial fashion ...

Acceptable:
In the abstract, the package at its fullest may include **the following:** the right to a hearing before a decision is made, the right to have the decision made in an unbiased and impartial fashion ...

In the example above, "the following" is verbiage that the author might nevertheless wish to retain so as to emphasize the list. The same result could be achieved by dropping the phrase and the colon and simply enumerating the items (the package may include (1) ...).

Here's a more fluid, more concise version:
In the abstract, the package at its fullest may include the right to a hearing before a decision is made, the right to have the decision made in an unbiased and impartial fashion....[9]

Colons & spaces	• *Boy on the Deck: From Hell to Atlantis*
One space after colon between title & subtitle or heading & subheading.	• The horizon was gone: smoke had swallowed the sea.
Likewise, one space after a colon in text.	

Miscellaneous colons

(a) time

(a) 11:47 p.m.

(b) ratios

(b) The women outnumbered men 3:1.
(*Or spell out:* three to one)

(c) analogies

(c) boy: Casabianca :: pirate : Blackbeard
(*Or spell out*: *Boy* is to *Casabianca* as *pirate* is to *Blackbeard*. (That is, *boy* & *pirate* are common nouns; *Casabianca* and *Blackbeard* are proper nouns — the individuals' names.)

Semicolons

Semicolons in a list or series
When a series of items is listed (not necessarily after a colon) AND the items contain internal commas, semicolons are used to clarify the separateness of the items.

If the items contain *no internal commas*, then they should be followed by commas, not semicolons.

The basic elements of administrative law include transparency and access to information; participation in administrative decisionmaking through the submission of information, analysis, and views; a requirement of a reasoned decision by the administrative decisionmaker; review of the decision for legality by an independent tribunal; and the application of the reviewing body of certain substantive principles such as means–ends rationality and proportionality.[10]

Semicolon between independent clauses
In this use, the semicolon functions as a heavy comma or a light period. It indicates that the material in the joined clauses is closely related, as they would

• The boy stood, hot, on burning deck; flames licked at his ankles and encircled his neck.

• In many instances, the administrative bodies in question have assumed a mixed public–private governance structure in which firms and NGOs participate along with representatives of states; this builds

be if joined by a conjunction, or that the second further explains the first.

on the longstanding approach exemplified by the tripartite governance structure of the ILO based on national delegations representing governments, employers, and labor.[11]

Semicolon between independent clauses when second clause is preceded by a transitional conjunctive adverb (e.g., accordingly, hence, however, indeed, therefore, thus) (For list of more, *see* I. GRAMMAR: Grammar Charts.)

If the semicolon here were a comma, these examples would demonstrate the error known as the ***"comma splice" (or "run-on" sentence)****: two independent clauses joined by a comma but missing a coordinating conjunction.*

- The boy stood, pensive, on the deck; **thus** he foresaw a cinder'd wreck.
- [I]t is highly likely that regulatory authorities ... will contact the local sponsors for information regarding Drug Watch postings[; **furthermore,**] [d]rug sponsors need prior notice of Drug Watch postings to prepare for these questions and to notify regulatory authorities and foreign affiliates as appropriate.[12]

Semicolon between two independent clauses when the second clause is preceded by a coordinating conjunction

This construction is perfectly permissible; the decision to use a semicolon rather than a comma may rest upon how it affects rhythm — that is, the longer pause signaled by the semicolon.

The boy stood, hot, on burning boards; **but** hotter were the pirate hoards.

Semicolon to clarify sentence parts to clearly separate an independent clause from a series that precedes it **when both use the same conjunction** or when one or the other includes internal commas or is particularly lengthy

Instead, several major international organizations claim interest **and** authority in the area of financial reporting; **and** over the past ten years, many of these public principals have come to endorse [the] IASB, thereby committing themselves to accept international accounting standards as authoritative rules.[13]

If the sentence above were a little simpler, a comma would have served the same purpose, and it would be acceptable for purposes of enhancing clarity even though the phrase that follows is not an independent clause:

Instead, several major international organizations claim interest **and** authority in the area of financial reporting, **and** have come to endorse the IASB....

Semicolons & appositives
Do not use a semicolon to separate a noun from an appositive noun phrase. Instead, use a comma, an em-dash, or a colon.

- The boy, **a lad one year past twelve,** was shaken by the pirates' yells.
- These he heard in tongues of three: **English, French, and Romany.**

Commas

Commas & Independent Clauses

A comma precedes the coordinating conjunction (and, or, nor, but, for, so, yet) joining two independent clauses.	You precede, and I'll follow.
Exception: if both clauses are very short, **(a)** the comma can go **or**	**(a)** You precede and I'll follow.
(b) the conjunction can go. (*See* II. PUNCTUATION: Elliptical Commas, below.) **NB:** This **(b)** is called a comma splice and is considered "incorrect"; but it is permissible when the clauses are very short and when it is stylistically intended.	**(b)** You precede, I'll follow.
NB: When a sentence has only one subject, it has only one independent clause, so ordinarily there is no comma preceding the conjunction.	He just shrugged and began to laugh.
Exception for emphasis or clarity: *See* II. PUNCTUATION: Semicolons — Semicolons to clarify sentence parts, above (second example); *see also* II. PUNCTUATION: Optional Commas — For Style, below.	

Commas & Series
of words, phrases, or clauses joined by a coordinating conjunction

(a) Place a comma after each item in a series to which the last item is joined by a coordinating conjunction (and, or, nor, but, yet). (The last comma is known as a *serial comma*. The better practice is not to drop it and thus to clarify that the last two items are not (or are) a pair.)	**(a)** • red, white, and blue • neither red, white, nor blue • For sandwiches, they brought liverwurst, tunafish, sprouts, peanut butter, and jelly. • [The agency] sent letters to chief executive officers of mutual funds, investment and commercial banks, rating agencies, **and** other user groups, inviting them to join....[14] • It incorporates by reference any decisions, rules, guidelines, measures or modifications, **or** agreements made under the Kyoto Protocol.[15]
(b) Do not use a comma if the items are separated by conjunctions.	**(b)** red **and** white **and** blue

Commas & Coordinate Adjectives
(words, phrases sequentially modifying a noun). See also II. PUNCTUATION: Hyphens, below.

A comma separates multiple coordinate adjectives (adjectives not linked by a coordinating conjunction) preceding the noun they modify, EXCEPT for the last adjective. Do not use a comma between the last adjective and the noun.	• The filthy, fatigued, emaciated racers threw what remained of their bodies across the finish line. • The nineties have witnessed a host of new, independent agencies.
Cf. Compound nouns: where adjectives end and the noun begins is ticklish when the noun is a nonhyphenated compound. *See also* II. PUNCTUATION: Commas and Coordinate Adjectives, Compound Modifiers, & Compound Nouns, below.	*Cf.* • European farmers could be predicted to resist the dictates of a mandatory [international regulatory regime].

Adjectives & adverbs:
No comma separates the adverb from the adjective it modifies.

In these examples,
modified noun
[ ] = *no comma*
→ = *adverb modifying this* → *adjective*

- The utterly filthy, frighteningly fatigued, emaciated **racers** threw what remained of their bodies across the finish line.
- The utterly[ ] → filthy, frighteningly[ ] → fatigued, emaciated **racers** threw what remained of their bodies across the finish line.

- occasionally absent, lay **board of directors**
- occasionally[ ] → absent, lay **board of directors**

Commas and Coordinate Adjectives, Compound Modifiers, & Compound Nouns

When the noun being modified is a composite of the last adjective(s) and the base noun (a **compound noun**), it is considered a single unit for purposes of punctuating the coordinate adjectives.

If the adjectives are part of a compound noun, do not use commas.

One test of whether one of several adjectives preceding a **compound noun** should be followed by a comma is to read it followed by *and*. If the *and* fits, then so would a comma.

This trick can sometimes help identify which adjective(s) are part of the compound noun itself. Start with the last adjective and work backward. When you hit an *and* that would work, then the term preceding it would likely not be part of the compound noun.

Remember: No comma after the last modifier, that abutting the (compound) noun. Here, "international."

What comprises the compound modifier depends on its context. (Does the article ever mention international regulatory regimes that are *not* treaty-based? The more consistent the term's use, the more recognizable it will be as a compound noun.

- marathon runners
- international regulatory regimes

The filthy[?] fatigued[?] emaciated[?] **marathon runners** threw what was left of their bodies across the finish line.
→ The filthy [and] fatigued [and] emaciated [~~and~~] **marathon runners** ...
→ The filthy, fatigued, emaciated **marathon runners** ...

This program is one of many complex [and] treaty-based [and] **international**[~~and~~] **regulatory**[~~and~~] **regimes**.

→ This program is one of many complex, treaty-based, **international regulatory regimes**.

OR?

This program is one of many complex [~~and~~] **treaty-based** [~~and~~] **international**[~~and~~] **regulatory**[~~and~~] **regimes**.

→ This program is one of many complex **treaty-based international regulatory regimes**.

Cf. Adjectives that are a part of a **compound modifier** are linked to one another by hyphens when the modifying term precedes the noun they modify. Compound modifiers can also be part of a compound noun. *See* II. PUNCTUATION: Hyphens, below.	• **third-party dispute-settlement mechanisms**

For a more comprehensive guide to hyphenating compound nouns, see Chicago Manual 7.90.

Commas (or no commas) & Parenthetical Elements

Parenthetical beginnings: Commas often signal a parenthetical comment — one that is inessential to the meaning of the main clause, but that enhances its meaning. Such a word or phrase that precedes the main clause is, in effect, a parenthetical beginning.

A comma follows an introductory, transitional conjunctive adverb (thus, therefore, however, nevertheless, moreover, still, accordingly, consequently. (For more, see I. Grammar: Grammar Charts, above.)	• **Thus,** Smith concluded that the statistics did not establish bias. • However, none agreed with him. • Nonetheless, no history of the negotiations was ever published.
NB: no comma after an initial coordinating conjunction	**NB:** Yet no history of the negotiations was ever published.
Cf. when the conjunction is followed by a parenthetical phrase	*Cf.* Yet, even though the scribes scribbled conscientiously throughout the process, no history of the negotiations was ever published.
NB: no comma after the (nonconjunctive) **adverbs** *thus* (meaning *in this way*) **or "however"** (meaning *howsoever, by whatever means*)	• **Thus** Smith concluded his lecture demonstrating that the statistics did not establish bias. • **However** hard he tried, he could not hide his fatigue.
Likewise, no commas for these adverbs with these meanings when used mid-sentence	• In **thus** abruptly concluding his lecture, Smith demonstrated that[,] **however** hard he had tried to hide it, even he could run out of steam.

For whether to use a comma after "that" used conjunctively when it is followed by a parenthetical clause, see II. PUNCTUATION: Optional Commas — For Style.

A comma follows a subordinate clause introduced with a subordinating conjunction (e.g. — *as, because, if, when, whether, while*).

For potential ambiguity in the use of *as* and *while* as subordinating conjunctions, see IV. USAGE & STYLE, below.

- When a sentence begins with a subordinate phrase or clause, it should be set off from the main clause with a comma.

- Because the history of discrimination has been largely superseded by the gains of the civil-rights movement, conservatives tend to believe that it has little application to current race relations.[16]

A comma follows other introductory words, phrases or clauses to ease reading:

(a) after **an adverb clause** (unnecessary if short),

(b) after **a prepositional phrase** (unnecessary if clear without),

or when otherwise needed, as

(c) after a very long introductory phrase or clause, or

(d) when misreading may result.

(a) Through the smoke and piratical din, he spied a tun that had once held gin.

(b)
- **In a flash,** before his eyes passed a life, though short, much prized.

- **For all the tea in China**[,] she would not go along with his nefarious scheme.

(c) Insofar as the functionalist argument is meant as a necessary argument, it rests on a conceptual fallacy.[17]

(d) To avoid misunderstanding, the writer should scrutinize her text for ambiguities.

Parenthetical Endings: USUALLY No Commas

A comma is usually unnecessary when the subordinate clause (introduced with a subordinating conjunction or preposition) **follows the main clause.**

Exception: A comma is tolerated when the author intends a deliberate pause, as when the subordinate clause is in effect parenthetical or nondefining ("oh, by the way") element.

See II. PUNCTUATION: Optional Commas — For Style.

- She would not go along with his nefarious scheme[ ] though he offered her all the tea in China.

- Conservatives tend to believe that the history of discrimination has little application to current race relations[ ] because that history has been largely superseded by the gains of the civil rights movement.[18]

NB: When the coordinating conjunction *for* can be substituted for *because*, the comma can — indeed, must — stay.

NB: Conservatives tend to believe that the history of discrimination has little application to current race relations[**, for**] that history has been largely superseded by the gains of the civil rights movement.[19]

Commas & No Commas: Defining* Versus Nondefining* Words, Phrases, Clauses

* These terms are used by H.W. Fowler, A Dictionary of Modern English Usage *(2d ed. 1965). They are alternatively described as "restrictive v. nonrestrictive" or "essential v. nonessential."*

Commas DO NOT set off a DEFINING element, one that defines the main clause and that the main clause cannot do without. It restricts the main clause in that way; it is essential to the sense of the main clause.

Commas DO set off NONDEFINING elements — Nondefining elements are those that do not "restrict," that are inessential to understanding the main clause, that the main clause can be read without. A nondefining phrase or clause is, in essence, a **parenthetical element**, enclosed in commas rather than in parentheses. It is an "oh, by the way" addition to the main clause, one dispensable to the meaning of the main clause.

Nondefining elements can be parenthetical beginnings (above), middles (enclosed in commas), or endings (preceded by a comma).

Commas & Nondefining (parenthetical) Elements

Commas set off transitional elements. (including conjunctive adverbs (e.g., thus, therefore, however, nevertheless, moreover, till, accordingly, consequently)).	• Smith concluded, **however,** that the statistics did not establish bias.
Commas set off **(a) nondefining adverbial phrases** (phrases or clauses that modify the action in the main clause), including **(b) absolute phrases** (that modify the whole clause or sentence that follows). *(Absolute constructions can look like improper dangling participles (is "it" doing the considering?); but they are not.)*	**(a)** • Smith concluded, **by no means easily,** that the statistics did not establish bias. • The bottom line is, **… if lots of new ideas come forward,** the agency will find that its officials in charge of the rulemaking will have to devote substantially more energy to responding to the ideas it has rejected.[20] **(b)** • Considering the price of gasoline, it is a wonder anyone drives anywhere anymore. • To avoid misunderstanding, the text should be carefully punctuated.

Commas set off nondefining appositives (noun, noun phrases).	**Nondefining:** My biological mother, Martha, lives in Iowa. *(I have only one biological mother. Her name is inessential to the sense of the sentence.)*
Commas set off a nondefining adjective phrase or clause, **(a)** generally (as with a participial phrase) **or** **(b)** when introduced by relative pronouns (e.g., who, which).	**(a)** The lad, **sensing courage surge from head to knees,** leapt leeward into the frothy seas. (*present participle*) **(b)** The lad, **who had but one life to give,** thought instead he would much rather live.
NB: Nondefining elements are never introduced with *that*.	**(b)** Governments and public agencies, **which** can use the specialized expertise solely for the purpose of regulation, will find maintaining such expertise more costly than will private actors, **who** can derive positive externalities from this expertise by also using it to improve products, processes, and so forth.[21]

NO Commas & Defining (essential) Elements

Do not use commas for defining appositives.	**Defining:** My dog Muesli is a mutt; my dog Alfie is an afghan. *(I have more than one dog. If this sentence is read without the dogs' names, it makes no sense. The names are essential to the sense of the sentence; it is restricted by or **defined** by that information.)*
Do not use commas for defining modifiers (adjective or adverbial phrases, clause), **(a)** generally (as with a participial phrase) **or**	**(a)** • The trial court sentenced the waitress **convicted of assaulting a mechanical bull** to community service. *(past participle)* • The pirate **wearing an eyepatch** eyed the lad. *(present participle)*

(b) introduced by relative pronouns (that, who).
(**Cf.** "which," which is nondefining and should be preceded by a comma.)

See also IV. USAGE & STYLE: Word Choice (that, which), below.

(b)

- The eyepatch **that the pirate wore** bespoke a past of guts and gore. *(relative pronoun)*

- The pirate **who wore an the eyepatch** eyed the lad. *(Only one pirate wore an eyepatch.)*

- The trial court sentenced the waitress **who had been convicted of assaulting a mechanical bull** to community service. *(The court sentenced not just any waitress, but the one convicted, etc.)*

- The results demonstrated that the high activity form of the gene did not manifest in violent propensities, even if the men had been mistreated as boys, while those with the low-active form of the gene **who had been mistreated** committed four times as many rapes, assaults, and robberies as the average.[22] *(No commas around the "who" clause because, if it's taken out, the parallel is incomplete and the sentence makes no sense.)*

Commas & Specialized Constructions

Contrasted Elements

E.g., not…, but …
not only…, but [also] …
on the one hand, … [on the other,] …

Commas are optional in these constructions. When the contrasted elements are short, commas may be unnecessary.

See also IV. USAGE & STYLE: Word Choice (not only … but [also]), below.

- The EU independent agencies parallel comitology, **not only** in the purported separation of politics or policy from administration**, but in** the masking of technocracy by national representation in a transnational body.[23]

- Such lawyers ought to accept this responsibility **not only** to avoid further liability **but also** to salvage their reputations.

NB: Although lawyers should want to accept this responsibility **on the one hand** to avoid liability, they should want to do so as well to safeguard their reputations and integrity.

Dates

(a) Month date, year. If the sentence continues after the year, a comma should follow the year.

(a) These remarks were made on **June 3, 2007,** at a conference on global warming.

Cf. a date used as an adjective (no comma).

Cf. The law was passed in the wake of the **September 11, 2001** terrorist attacks.

(b) Day month year. No comma unless required by some other rule (as when followed by a parenthetical phrase).

(b) These remarks were made on **3 June 2007** at a conference on global warming.

(c) Month year. No comma unless required by some other rule.

(c) These remarks were made in **June 2007** at a conference on global warming.

Locations & Subparts

Commas set off each element of

(a) an address or location

(b) a text

(a) Japanese Americans were evacuated to Manzanar Relocation Camp, Manzanar, California, among other forbidding locations.

(b) Surprisingly, the Court held that this exercise of eminent domain did not violate Article Three, Section Nine, of the Constitution.

Abbreviations of Degrees, Offices, & Other Identifying Designations

Commas set off abbreviations of degrees, offices, or corporate designation:

(a) Commas separate a person's name from her professional degree or office or a corporation's name from the designation of incorporation.

(a)
• John Terborgh, Ph.D., was awarded a MacArthur Grant.

• The Ninth Circuit introduced the term "substantial participation" in the Everett System, Inc., case.

(b) No commas separate a person's name from Jr. or Sr.

(b) Jim Bob Jr. looks just like his daddy.

Commas & Citations in Footnote Text

BLUEBOOK R. 1.1(b), 2.2(b)

(a) If a citation supports only a portion of a footnote sentence, set it off from the text it supports with commas.

(a) Although press accounts at the time highlighted Jackson's "loaded gun" metaphor, ***see, e.g., Death Asked for Nazi Leaders*** [sic], ***Guilty as Hitler, Says Jackson***, N.Y. TIMES, July 27, 1946, at 4, ... none ... connected this Jackson "loaded gun" at Nuremberg to the "loaded weapon" that he had ... warned against in *Korematsu*, ***see Korematsu v. United States***, **323 U.S. 214, 246 (1944) (Jackson, J., dissenting) (noting the majority opinion effectively validated the principle of racial discrimination, which would "then lie[ ] about like a loaded weapon").**

(b) If more than one source supports that portion of the sentence, separate the two citations with a semicolon, but follow the citations with a comma before continuing with text.

(b) Although press accounts at the time highlighted Jackson's "loaded gun" metaphor, ***see e.g.,*** **[source one]**; **[source two]**, ... none ... connected this Jackson "loaded gun" at Nuremberg to the "loaded weapon" that he had ... warned against in *Korematsu*, **[source three]**.

(c) If a citation directly supports the entire sentence, set it off from the text with a period.

(c) Press accounts at the time highlighted Jackson's "loaded gun" metaphor. ***See, e.g., Death Asked for Nazi Leaders*** [sic], ***Guilty as Hitler, Says Jackson***, N.Y. TIMES, July 27, 1946, at 4.[24]

Optional Commas

For Clarity

If an independent clause has multiple verbs, commas may be necessary to differentiate a pair or clusters of actions from a separate one.

These officials communicate **and** meet informally, **and** may accomplish a good more than in formal sessions.

For Style

A comma may be inserted between an independent clause and a phrase that follows when an emphatic pause is desirable (as when the writer wishes to emphasize contrast (*but*)).	• These considerations are less frequently proffered, but are vital in the context of the Founding.[25]
A comma may set off a subordinate clause following the main clause *only* if the writer intends the information that follows to be inessential (nondefining) to the comprehension of the sentence clause. Sometimes it's a hard call: then **the default is no comma.**	• The history of discrimination has little application to current race relations**, because** history cannot be changed. • Conservatives tend to believe that the history of discrimination has little application to current race relations[ ] **because** that history has been largely superseded by the gains of the civil rights movement.[26]
Adjectival, adverbial phrases & clauses follow the same guidelines: Is the phrase that follows essential to understanding the noun? Then no commas. Inessential? Then use commas.	• Successive waves of lawsuits **targeting the small and the weak** were brought. *[defining participial phrase, essential to understanding which lawsuits were brought]* • Successive waves of lawsuits[,] targeting rich and poor, strong and weak, living and dead[,] were brought. *[nondefining participial phrase, inessential to understanding the main point about a succession of lawsuits.]*

Commas after "that" used as a conjunction

"That" used as a conjunction connects a noun or verb to a phrase or clause that completes it.

(a) When a parenthetical phrase or clause intervenes between "that" and the remainder of the phrase or clause it introduces, commas ordinarily precede and follow the intervening words.

(a)
• Early in his film, *An Inconvenient Truth* [citation omitted], Al Gore identifies an assumption that**, if believed,** leads most to think that "global warming" cannot really be a problem.
• But like Gore's point about man's effect on global warming, these scholars argued that**, whether or not "technical,"** this law was in fact producing an increasingly significant, and largely unintended, effect on the growth and spread of culture and knowledge.[27]

(b) Nonetheless, some writers habitually drop the first comma without ill effect. The resulting absence of symmetry aside, so long as the practice is consistent and results in no ambiguity, it is perfectly acceptable.

(b) One can only comment that **if such a refuge was open to the Romans,** it is much more available to our own people.[28]

An elliptical comma can take the place of a missing element in

(a) a parallel construction or

(a) The mast was a matchstick; the crows nest, ~~was~~ aflame.

(b) parallel items in a series.

(b) To cover her tuition, financial aid contributed 60 percent; a merit scholarship, 30 percent; and an anonymous donor, 10 percent.

(c) When the series or construction is clear without the comma, the comma may be omitted.

(c) To cover her tuition, financial aid contributed 60 percent, a merit scholarship 30 percent, and an anonymous donor 10 percent.

(d) A potential problem is confusing the construction with an appositive.

(d) Typical projects and ideas are the new *lex mercatoria*, European and global restatements (Principles), the new natural law.[29]
Are the Principles the new natural law? If these are not the same thing, the elliptical comma is not enough
→ **and** the new natural law

The "tag" comma separates the statement from the question it introduces (even when the question is not in quotes).

One way of looking at the question is to ask, what would they have suffered if we had not intervened.

Hyphens

See also V. CONVENTIONS: Spelling Conventions — Prefixes & Hyphens, below.

Hyphens & Compound Nouns

See Chicago Manual §7.90

A compound noun consists of more than one word used as a single term.

(a) Sometimes compound nouns are joined (lawgiver); sometimes they are hyphenated (mix-up); sometimes they are neither joined nor hyphenated (rule of law). Sometimes they are nouns + nouns; sometimes they are modifiers + nouns.

(a)
- sixty-five-year-old
- sexual offender
- independent contractor
- law review
- dispute settlement

(b) Familiar compound nouns may be in the dictionary. First check Webster's and Black's.

(b)
- materialmen (Black's)
- law merchant (Webster's)
- website (Webster's)
- policyholder (Webster's)
- business-judgment rule (Black's)

(c) Some compounds are fused by convention by scholars within a particular field. Such conventions are acceptable if comprehensible and consistently used.

(c)
- policymaking
- rulemaking
- decisionmaking (*but see* Black's "decision-making responsibility")

Sometimes it is hard to tell whether a noun is a compound or whether it is modified by a compound.

See II. PUNCTUATION: Hyphens — Hyphenation & Compound Modifiers, below.

Cf. **en dashes** between equivalent entities or to show duality	• a mixed public–private governance structure • business–NGO partnerships • principal–agent relationship • means–ends rationale • normative–prescriptive debate • He is CEO–CFO of the company
N.B. But check WEBSTER'S.	**N.B.** cost-benefit analysis

Hyphenation & Compound Modifiers
(a.k.a. phrasal adjectives)

General rule: Hyphenate two or more words used as a single adjective (compound modifier). Academics (including lawyers) tend to drop hyphens when the compound modifier is presumed to be familiar to the reader (such as a legal compound noun or term of art). Nonetheless, **the better practice** (because it is most likely to prevent ambiguity) **is to hyphenate all parts of the modifying term.**	*Compound modifier + noun* • fair-trade + coffee • treaty-based + authorities • a states-rights + approach • sixty-five-year-old + males • antisocial-personality-disorder + patients • subject-matter + jurisdiction • law-review + article • intellectual-property + rights • common-law + marriage
Cf. **a modified compound noun** When more than one modifier precedes a compound noun, whether and what to hyphenate depends on which of those terms modify that noun and which are instead functionally part of it. *Test:* Does the questioned term modify the final noun or the term preceding it? [Brackets mark the term modified. →] If the questioned term modifies the term that follows it, it's part of a com-	• international regulatory regime • hospital price discrimination • dispute-settlement procedure • less-developed nations *Test:* • international [regulatory regime] (*"international" does not modify "regulatory," but "regime," so no hyphen.*) • hospital → [price discrimination] (*"hospital" does not modify price, but discrimination (specifically, price discrimination), so no hyphen.*)

pound modifier (needs a hyphen), not part of a compound noun (usually no hyphen).

But see Exception: Unmistakable adverbs, below.

BUT:
- less → [developed] nations → less-developed nations
- *Cf.* less → [meaningful attention] was paid to those nations
- dispute → [settlement] procedure → dispute-settlement procedure

---

Some compound modifiers have fused, as have many compound nouns.
Check (WEBSTER'S & BLACK'S).
See also V. CONVENTIONS: Spelling Conventions — Prefixes & Hyphens, below.

- commonsense approach
- courthouse steps

(a) Hyphenate a compound noun that functions as a compound modifier (or as part of one), even if the compound noun is not hyphenated standing alone.

(a) *compound noun → compound modifier + noun*
- risk assessment → actuarial-risk-assessment analysis
- sexual offender → sexual-offender-registration laws
- religious text → religious-text-based education
- dispute settlement → dispute-settlement procedure

(b) Hyphenate any compound modifier that is in fact part of a compound noun, even when these seem familiar to a legally trained reader.

(b)
- business-judgment rule

EXCEPTIONS: Signals that a word is part of a compound modifier make the hyphen unnecessary. Such compound modifiers may consist of proper nouns (and as such are capitalized), adverbs ending in –ly, words in quotation marks (such as introduced terms of art), words linked with an en-dash, or familiar phrases joined by conjunctions or prepositions.

Exception: Do not hyphenate a compound modifier consisting of proper nouns, including the names of ethnic or other subgroups (because the capital letters signal that the term is a compound).

- Nobel Prize winner Al Gore
- University of North Carolina law professor
- African American population
- Japanese American civil liberties cases
- the Driving While Black phenomenon
- a Creative Commons license

Cf. Anglo-American heritage (WEBSTER'S)

Exception: Do not hyphenate a compound modifier whose terms include other signals of the cluster, such as apostrophes, quotation marks, en-dashes, or foreign terms (even when these are not italicized).

- arm's length transaction
- the "health flexible spending arrangement" model
- a mixed public–private governance structure
- an exercise of in personam jurisdiction
- *fois gras* production
- per capita benefits

Cf. laissez-faire economics (WEBSTER'S)

Exception: Unmistakable adverbs

(a) Do not hyphenate -ly adverbs that modify the next word in a compound modifier.

(b) Do not use a hyphen after "most," "least," "often," or "very" in a compound modifier.

(c) Do not use a hyphen after "more" or "less" when used unambiguously as adverbs rather than as adjectives.

(a)
- internationally traded products
- sustainably harvested timber
- sexually violent predator statutes

(b)	**(c)**
• most viable alternative	• the more general point
• least viable alternative	*Cf.* several more-general
• very complex question	points
• often unnerved clientele	• a less notable change
	Cf. less-notable change

Exception: When the compound modifier is unmistakably a phrase, as when joined by a conjunction or preposition, the hyphen(s) can be dropped (unless the phrase can be misread without the hyphen(s)).

- state of the art → state of the art technology
- health and safety regulations
- conflict of laws issues

Cf.
- food- and plant-health safety standards

Other adverbs & hyphens

(a) Hyphenate a compound modifier **preceding** the term modified,

(a)
- Well-read and well-bred, he turned heads.
- a pervasive and well-supported theory
- the much-recognized theory
- More-educated people tend to have better health care overall than **(b)** those who are less educated.

(b) but do not hyphenate a compound modifier **following** the term modified (because misreading is unlikely).

(b)
- He was well bred and well read.
- The theory is much recognized.

Hyphenate successive compound modifiers that share a term (but only when a common term ends each). For use of hyphens with prefixes and suffixes, see also V. CONVENTIONS: Spelling Conventions — Prefixes, Suffixes, & Hyphens.	• a thirty- to forty-year period • fifty-eight- to sixty-eight-year-old judges • under- or overpaid executives • upper- rather than lower-case letters • GPL- and Creative Commons-licensed software • mid- to late twentieth century *["Twentieth century" is treated here as a compound noun; "late" takes no hyphen; "mid" needs one to clarify the shared term.]* **Cf.** hard-knock and hard-rock lifestyles.

Hyphens & Titles

These vary: check WEBSTER's and conventions for the particular organization.	• Vice President Cheney (*See* WEBSTER's.) • Vice-Consul (WEBSTER's) • Vice-Chancellor (WEBSTER's) • the Secretary-General of the UN

Hyphens & Numbers

(a) Hyphenate numbers from twenty-one to ninety-nine; likewise ordinals.	**(a)** twenty-one to ninety-nine; twenty-first to ninety-ninth
(b) Hyphenate spelled-out fractions.	**(b)** At the 1787 Philadelphia Convention, the northern and southern states agreed upon a compromise whereby three-fifths of the slave population would be counted for purposes of apportioning members of the federal House of Representatives.
(c) Do not use hyphens for numerals or symbols used in compound modifiers or for numbers indicating a percentage.	**(c)** • an $18 billion agreement, a $55 million debt • a three percent raise, a 100% loss

Hyphenation at the End of a Line of Text

In page proofs, a word with seven or more letters can be divided, but not if doing so leaves a syllable of a single letter standing alone.

En Dash

The en dash is so called because it is the width of a capital N (no spaces on either side).

En Dashes & Numbers

(a)(i) Use an en dash for ranges — pages, years, sections, etc. The en-dash means "through."

> **NB**: Unlike page spans, **spans of years** should include all numerals; in text, do not use the dash, but spell out "through."

(a)(i)
- pp. 103–04
- Justice Sandra Day O'Connor's tenure (1981–2005) was on the short end of that of the justices sitting at the time of her retirement.

NB: Justice Sandra Day O'Connor's tenure, **from** 1981 **through** 2005, was on the short end of that of the justices sitting at the time of her retirement.

(a)(ii) If the items are separate but sequential, separate with commas.

(a)(ii) Fed. R. Evid. 402, 403.

(b) En dashes are particularly useful in citing spans in statutory sections, which might use hyphens for other purposes,

(b)
- 5 U.S.C. app. II §§ 10–11
- 21 C.F.R. § 314.430(b)–(d)

or

(c) after a date to show that the span is continuing

(c) The tenure of the sitting justices ranges from less than a year for Justice Alito (2006–) to thirty-four years for Justice Stevens (1975–).

En Dashes & Words

Use an **en dash**

(a) between equivalent entities or concepts (compounds of equivalents),

(a)
- a so-called statutory–adjudicatory model
- public–private law
- the U.S.–E.U. Mutual Recognition Agreement
- domestic–international dichotomy
- East–West cultural tension
- agent–principal link
- means–ends analysis, risk–benefit analysis
- normative–prescriptive debate
- employer–employee relationship

Exceptions: hyphenated compounds included in WEBSTER'S

Exceptions:
- nation-state
- cost-benefit

(b) in place of a hyphen in compounds with elements of more than one word,	**(b)** • The Republican Party–led coalition • the Paris Club–initiated process
(c) between any prefix and a nonhyphenated (open) compound of two or more words,	**(c)** • pre–Civil War • non–Paris Club claimants • non–Article III courts • non–social scientist • post–World War I
(d) in place of a solidus (slash) indicating a hybrid), **and**	**(d)** • a Sri Lankan/Korean joint venture → a Sri Lankan–Korean joint venture • U.S.–Korean agreement • the United States' global–political agenda • the IMF–World Bank
(e) in place of a hyphen when a hyphen would lead to ambiguity, such as linking hyphenated or open compound nouns.	**(e)** • quasi-legislative–quasi-judicial body
(f) For abbreviation of terms joined by an en dash, use a hyphen.	**(f)** • Principal–Agent Theory (P-A)

Em Dash

(so called because it is the width of a capital M) (no spaces on either side)

Em dashes are accepted in formal writing and are useful for these (often overlapping) purposes:	• The em dash can come mid-sentence—like this—in which case there are two, as there would be two parentheses. • Or a single em dash may separate the end of the sentence from the rest—like this.
Em dash as a textual parenthetical The text between em dashes (as it would be placed parenthetically) can be an aside, a clarification, or an explanation of the main sentence.	[The decision] holds that a right of access and a right to defense arise at the moment in which the facts—in this case, negligence—giving rise to the adverse decision—denial of the remission of import duties—are determined.[30]

Em dash to clarify the separation of parenthetical elements otherwise signaled by commas. Parenthetical material set off by em dashes is often more clearly parenthetical than material set off by commas; because the latter has more uses (such as a series list), the comma's signal can initially be more ambiguous than that of an em dash.

Em dash as an informal colon, introducing an appositive word or phrase signaling (without saying) *i.e.* or *namely*, or signaling (without saying) *e.g.*

Less clear:

These patterns can result in repetition of sequences of movements, for example, stabbing repeatedly, and may be part of uncontrolled action patterns rather than rage.[31]

More clear:

These patterns can result in repetition of sequences of movements—for example, stabbing repeatedly—and may be part of uncontrolled action patterns rather than rage.

[T]he European [c]ourts have recognized the legitimate and unitary nature of the composite proceedings in the context of two areas, revenues—remissions of import duties, customs exemptions, et cetera—and expenditures—Community subsidies—that are characteristic of a public power.[32]

Em dashes: Caveats
- Avoid nesting independent clauses between em dashes unless they are quite short.
- Overuse of the dash can lend a tone of hysteria to prose.

Apostrophes

To form possessive of a singular noun:

(a) Add **'s**

(b) unless name ending in **s** ends in an "eez" sound.

(c) To indicate the possessive of a plural noun ending in **s**, add an apostrophe.

(d) **Acceptable exception for words ending in "s":** follow pronunciation.

(e) Use apostrophe to indicate plural letters only when the letter is the same size and in the same font as the letter itself.

(a) Blunderbus**'s** contribution to the perennial problems of international law stimulates little insight.

(b) Achilles' contribution to the perennial problems of international law are legion.

(c) most cartels' ability to police their members

(d) Blunderbus's contribution

(d) Albert Camus' *The Plague*

(d) Achilles' heel

(d) for goodness' sake

(e) Mind your own p's and q's.

Cf.

(e) Mind your own Ps and Qs.

(e) Mind your own *ps* & *qs*.

Possessives & gerunds Gerunds are nouns. As such, they require that the actor own up to the action, just as he would own up to his hat.	• The **executive's hat** was not right for the occasion. • The potential impropriety here was in the **executive's** "picking and choosing" between its international commitments. • The most glaring *faux pas* was the CEO's wearing his baseball cap to the board meeting. *Emphasis is on the wearing of the baseball cap.*
Cf. participles, which look like gerunds, but which are adjectives, not nouns. So the noun modified would not be possessive and would sport no apostrophe. *See also* I. GRAMMAR: Verbals, above.	***Cf.*** Most irreverent was the CEO wearing his baseball cap to the board meeting. *Emphasis is on the CEO.*
Possessives and "of": a possessive "s" is a permissible idiom.	This dog of Jack's. That elephantine nose of his.

Parentheses ( )

Parenthetical text (in the nature of an aside): If the text within the parentheses is grammatically complete, include terminal punctuation within the parentheses. If not, punctuation is outside the closing parenthesis.	• (So they say**.**) • [T]he state is constrained not only by other states and by supranational organizations but also by non-state organizations (e.g., NGOs), communities (e.g., religious groups), and powerful private players (e.g., multinational corporations).[33]
Parentheses to introduce abbreviations: Use (without quotation marks) when the abbreviation is first introduced, but not thereafter.	The predecessor to the Organization for Economic Co-operation and Development (OECD), the Organization for European Economic Cooperation (OEEC), was created in April 1948. The OECD, like the OEEC …
Parentheses surround numerals in a textual list.	In the abstract, the package at its fullest may include (1) the right to a hearing before a decision is made, (2) the right to have the decision made in an unbiased and impartial fashion, (3) the right to know the basis of the decision so that it can be contested, (4) the right to reasons for the official's decision, and (5) the right to a decision that is reasonably justified by all relevant legal and factual considerations.[34]

When the list is blocked off from the text, though, the parentheses can be dispensed with, but the numbers should be followed by periods**.**

See also V. CONVENTIONS: Lists, below.

In the abstract, the package at its fullest may include the following:

1. The right to a hearing before a decision is made.
2. The right to have the decision made in an unbiased and impartial fashion.
3. The right to know the basis of the decision so that it can be contested.
4. The right to reasons for the official's decision.
5. The right to a decision that is reasonably justified by all relevant legal and factual considerations.

Slash /
(a.k.a. Solidus or Virgule)

In formal writing DO NOT USE the slash or solidus between words, whether

(a) to indicate a composite,
    (i) substitute an en dash
    or
    (ii) reconfigure with hyphens.

or

(b) to indicate and/or, either/or, or the like.
    (i) Although the construction "or … or both" is wordy, it is preferable to the justifiably much-maligned "and/or," which is neither here nor there.
    (ii) The "or both" can often be dropped.)

or

(c) to mean "per."

(a)(i) Sri Lankan/Korean joint venture
    → Sri Lankan–Korean joint venture

(a)(ii) Heavy up/downloaders inside the commercial sphere are prone to suit.
    → Heavy up- or down-loaders inside …

(b)(i) Domestic law is a controlling source of law for administrative agencies implementing global law [and/or] **or** acting as a part of global administrative structures**, or both**.[35]

(b)(ii) Domestic law is a controlling source of law for administrative agencies implementing global law **or** acting as a part of global administrative structures.

(c)   How many miles **per** gallon does this hybrid get?

NB:
It is acceptable to use the slash between numbers or abbreviations, particularly when these are the official names of the event or entity.

NB:
- The terrorist attacks on September 11, 2001 are commonly referred to as **9/ll**
- **GATT/WTO** negotiating rules
- **HIV/AIDS**
- 24/7 news coverage
Cf.
- the IMF–World Bank
  See II. PUNCTUATION: En dashes and Words, above.

Question Marks

Question marks follow questions, not statements. "Whether" initiates statements.

Whether a question mark punctuates a statement of the issue depends on whether it stated or asked.

- Does Ms. Ledbetter have a viable claim under Title VII when she failed to file a complaint within 180 days of her first discrepant paycheck?
- Whether Ms. Ledbetter has a viable Title VII claim for pay discrimination when she failed to file a complaint within 180 days of her first discrepant paycheck is the question before the Court.

Quotation Marks

Quotation Marks as Signals

Terms of art:

(a) When a term of art is introduced for the first time, it should be distinguished with quotation marks. Thereafter, it can be used without the marks.

(a) "Gatekeepers" are defined as reputational intermediaries who provide verification and certification to investors.[36]

(b) Similarly, terms introduced by distinguishing words or phrases such as *defined, signed, the expression, termed, called* (but not *so-called*) should be placed in quotes.

(b)
- defined as the "gay gene"
- the so-called gay gene

(c) Coined words or phrases can be signaled as such with quotation marks.

(c) the "minilateral" setting of the EC[37]

(d) Some style manuals permit terms of art in *italics* rather than in quotation marks. This is always appropriate for unfamiliar foreign terms. For terms as terms, though, the default should be quotation marks.

(d) For some, function is synonymous with purpose and *causa finalis*.

Exception: Numerous terms introduced as variables or as components of upcoming graphs or tables may be italicized to eliminate the extraneous "noise" of quotation marks.

Exception:
Constraints are captured with variables … that address both information and beliefs: *uncertainty about preferences* (that is, uncertainty regarding what the other state partners' preferences are), *uncertainty about behavior* (not being able to decipher easily whether the other state partners are cooperating or defecting), and *uncertainty about the state of the world* (that is, uncertainty regarding the consequences of cooperation — who will benefit the most, et cetera.)[38]

Style:

(a) A word or phrase may be emphasized (or irony implied) by being placed in quotations marks ("scare quotes").

(a) [G]lobal legal pluralism would find an ideal testing ground for the otherwise academic question whether nonstate normative orders can be recognized as "law."[39]

(b) Likewise, the author's specialized usage may be distinguished by being put in quotes.

(b) [Although] "race" and "ethnicity" are difficult and contentious terms to define, this article treats them both as social constructs with overlapping meanings.[40]

Quotations Marks vis-à-vis Placement of Other Punctuation (and Footnote Numbers)

Quotations within quotations: Start with double. Then use single, then double within the single, and so forth.

That the corporation's counsel chose to "not reconsider, or 'second guess,' the accountant's judgments" was irresponsible.

Exception: When the language quoted by more than one party is **identical**, it is enough to indicate this with verbal signals, and the single quotes within the double ones can be dropped.

Exception: " …" (quoting …)

Quotation marks & other punctuation:

(a) Periods & commas go inside quotation marks.

(a) He said, "I choose not to reconsider or, as you term it, 'second guess' your judgments."

(b) Semicolons & colons go outside quotation marks.

(b) He said, "I choose not to reconsider or, as you term it, 'second guess' your judgments"; nevertheless, he was evidently dubious of their soundness.

(c) Question marks and exclamation marks stay inside if they are part of the text; outside if they are part of the framing.

(c) Was it not foolhardy that he said, "I choose not to reconsider or, as you term it, 'second guess' your judgments!"?

Placement of punctuation vis-à-vis footnote numbers: All punctuation except the dash goes inside the footnote number.

The brave new world of genomics, spurred on by the Human Genome Project,[1] presents tantalizing possibilities for developments in criminal law as well as advances in medicine and understanding disease.

The brave new world of genomics—spurred on by the Human Genome Project[1]—presents tantalizing possibilities for developments in criminal law as well as advances in medicine and understanding disease.[41]

III

Quotations

Introducing Quotations

The quotation should be integrated into the text as seamlessly as possible. The less material quoted, the greater its impact. Block quotations are least carefully read (if, indeed, read at all); short quotations integrated into the writer's sentence are most easily assimilated by the reader.

Quotations in the Context of a Textual Sentence

(for quotations of forty-nine words or fewer)

When the quotation is syntactically integrated into the text, do not place a comma or colon between the text and the quotation unless the syntax of the framing sentence requires it.

"Syntactic integration" includes introducing the quotation with *that* in lieu of a more formal introduction followed by a comma. *See* **(a)** below.

Any initial capitalization of the quotation is modified accordingly.

- They questioned whether "priority [is] given to offenders or to victims with respect to fairness."[1]
- [T]he Final Communiqué for the Summit stated that "[g]overnments should help promote sustainable practices by taking environmental factors into account when providing financing support for investment in infrastructure and equipment."[2]

NB: when the writer wishes to quote only part of an infinitive or prepositional phrase — or even a commonly known phrase — that element should be kept intact and changes made bracketed within the quotation.

Less seamless:
The objective is **to keep "in mind** the standards prescribed in the international protocols."

More seamless:
The objective is **"[to keep] in mind** the standards prescribed in the international protocols."

A quotation that is a complete sentence formally introduced by text should begin with a capital letter, bracketed if the sentence is not quoted from the beginning.

(a)

(a) A **comma** follows the framing phrase when the phrase is not an independent clause **and** it is introduced by such words as "says," "replies," "asks," "noted," "observed," "indicated," or "concluded."

- In 1997, for example, the Final Communiqué for the Summit **stated,** "Governments should help promote sustainable practices by taking environmental factors into account when providing financing support for investment in infrastructure and equipment."[3]

- As the Final Communiqué for the Summit put it, "Governments should help promote sustainable practices by taking environmental factors into account when providing financing support for investment in infrastructure and equipment."

- They **asked,** "[I]s priority given to offenders or to victims with respect to fairness?"

(b) A **colon** or a period follows the framing sentence only when it is an independent clause.

(b) The Scouts' Supreme Court brief emphasized that boy scouts are a special case: "Troops are incontrovertibly small, closely knit groups."

Paragraph indentation

For quotations that are run into text, original paragraph structure is not indicated.

Block Quotes

Bluebook R. 5

A quotation of **fifty words or more** is quoted as a block. Both margins are indented, the quotation is single-spaced. In a law review, the quotation font is a smaller size than that of the text.

Paragraph indentation

In block quotes, indicate the beginning of a paragraph by indenting the first line.

The rules for introducing shorter quotations apply as well to block quotes:

Block quotes may be formally introduced by an independent clause that concludes with a **colon** or **period**. (*See* (b)(ii), above).

Commenting on the funding change, Robert Herz, FASB Chairman since 2002, spoke words that in the pre-Enron era would have struck many … as pure heresy**:**

> [W]e need the support, understanding, and partnership of politicians and government officials in helping [to] ensure that accounting standard setting is not subject to inappropriate constituent influence. [quotation continues][4]

Commenting on the funding change, Robert Herz, FASB Chairman since 2002, spoke words that in the pre-Enron era would have struck many … as pure heresy**.**

> [W]e need the support, understanding, and partnership of politicians and government officials. [quotation continues][4]

A third option is to run the block quote into the introductory sentence, as by linking it with "that."

Do not inject either a comma or a colon after "that" (unless the former is called for by the syntax of the quote).

If the quotation introduced by "that" is a sentence (or more), the initial capital should be in lower case and bracketed, as it would be if not quoted as a block.

Commenting on the funding change, Robert Herz, FASB Chairman since 2002, said that

> we need the support, understanding, and partnership of politicians and government officials. [quotation continues]

Miller, Redding, and Bahnson said that

> [a]lthough working at the SEC may provide an intangible benefit, it seems unlikely that the [SEC] would be able to consistently locate, hire, train, and retain people. [quotation continues][5]

Single-Character Insertions & Omissions; [sic]

BLUEBOOK R. 5

Brackets: Changes in or insertions of punctuation, letters, or words (e.g., capitals to lower case, singular to plural, grammatical corrections) should be in brackets.

Ammar observes that "[b]y providing quality and caring representation[,] … we are reversing the way legal services have traditionally been provided to the poor."[6]

(a) Indicate **omission of letters or punctuation** with an empty bracket. **[ ]**

(a) "[These words] reveal[ ] logical connections."

(b) Errors: Rather than use **[sic]** for errors in the original, fix it in brackets, unless the author intends to flag the error or its irony.

(b)
- **Not:** Her prose is best described as obfusticating [sic].
- **But:** Her prose is best described as obfus[ ]cating.
- *See, e.g., Death Asked for Nazi Leaders* [**sic**], *Guilty as Hitler, Says Jackson*, N.Y. TIMES, July 27, 1946, at 4.

Unconventional material in quotation: Leave unconventional spelling, capitalization, numerals, symbols, etc. as in the original rather than distract by bracketing a change to follow manual convention.

The queen wrote in her diary, "Sir Walter's behaviour is extraordinary. He hath now laid his cloak on the mud before our royal feet 3 or 4 times altogether."

Textual Omissions

Indicate the omission of one or more words within a quotation with an **ellipsis** (three periods separated by spaces).

Do not use automatic ellipses offered by word-processing software. Indicate them thus: #.#.#.#

Original:

Likewise, while rejecting Brainerd Currie's own parochial *application* of his governmental interest approach (where the local party generally has its law applied), a cosmopolitan framework is firmly grounded in an expanded notion of governmental interests. Indeed, as courts consider multiple community affiliations and develop hybrid rules for resolving multistate disputes, they do so, not because they are *ignoring* the policy choices of their home state, but because they are *effectuating* their state's broader interest in taking part in a global community. Thus, a cosmopolitan approach is ultimately moored to an expanded conception of how governments must operate in an interconnected world.

[One or more paragraphs elided here.]

A cosmopolitan approach to cross-border adjudication, therefore, allows courts to engage in a dialogue with each other concerning the appropriate definition of community affiliation and the appropriate scope of prescriptive jurisdiction. In addition, it asks courts to develop intersystemic norms, thereby harnessing the generative potential of transnational litigation. Whereas treaties and other formal instruments of international law-making are cumbersome and slow to adjust to changing technologies or social conditions, transnational common-law adjudication is far more dynamic. As a result, international private-law litigation can serve public values as forums for debates about community affiliation and as generators of new common-law international norms.[7]

NB: An ellipsis rarely begins a quotation.

Exceptions:

(a) More than one paragraph is being quoted and material has been excluded from the beginning of the second paragraph, as here. *See* BLUEBOOK R.5.1(a)(iii).

(b) The quotation begins mid-sentence with a capitalized word (such as a proper noun). *See* CHICAGO MANUAL 11.65; *but see* BLUEBOOK R. 5.3 (not recognizing this exception).

For single paragraphs, partial single paragraphs, or sentences, begin at the beginning of the sentence or indicate it is not the beginning with a bracketed capital.

If one or more sentences (within the same paragraph) are omitted after the end of a quoted sentence **and** the quotation is then resumed, indicate omission with an ellipsis after the terminal punctuation of the preceding sentence.

NB: This is the ONLY instance in which a period will precede the ellipsis (i.e., no space between the last letter of the sentence and the ellipsis).

Redacted:

(a)

    … [C]ourts consider[ing] multiple community affiliations and develop[ing] hybrid rules for resolving multistate disputes … do so, not because they are *ignoring* the policy choices of their home state, but because they are *effectuating* their state's broader interest in taking part in a global community.…

    …

    … [I]nternational private law litigation can serve public values as forums for debates about community affiliation and as generators of new common law international norms.

(b)

"… Cole was a merry old soul, and a merry old soul was he."

Use an ellipsis at the end ONLY if a single quoted sentence is cut off before its end, yet it can still be read as a sentence. Then use a SPACE + ellipsis.

"[C]ourts consider multiple community affiliations and develop hybrid rules for resolving multistate disputes...."

If the quoted material is a phrase that cannot be mistakenly read as a sentence, do not use an ellipsis.

Cf.

Hybrid rules have been developed for "resolving multistate disputes."

Exception: When the quoted phrase is a deliberate fragment, use a terminal ellipsis but no period.

Exception:

I cannot remember what comes after "These are the times that try ..." Is the next part about our patience?

IV

Usage & Style

Usage

This section is about appropriate word choice. The style of legal writing in general, and of law journals in particular, is a formal style. Awareness of tone, of nuance, and of potential ambiguity are as important to the writer's choice of a written vocabulary as are words' meanings. Slang may have its rare, stylistic place; but less-deliberate, informal, or faddish usage probably does not.

Indispensable resources in addition to these few listings are WEBSTER'S and GARNER'S MODERN LEGAL USAGE.

Word Choice: Use & Misuse

For how a verb's being transitive (vt) or intransitive (vi) affects its use, see I. GRAMMAR: Verbs, above.

---

affect, effect

- **to affect (vt)** = to have an influence on
- **to effect (vt)** = to bring about
- **affect (n)** = "observable manifestations of a subjectively experienced emotion" (WEBSTER'S)
- **effect (n)** = that which is brought about

The **effect** of his proposal was as plain as the nose on her face: her **affect** was strained, so strongly did those words **affect** her, and they ultimately **effect**ed her acquiescence.

The mayor's proclamation was stated publicly and **effected** the public's reliance on its promise.

---

afterward(s), backward(s), forward(s), toward(s), northward(s)

The U.S. practice is to drop the "s." The British prefer the terminal "s" for the adverb, but drop it for the adjective form of these words.[1]

The **forward** flank moved **toward** the north, **backward** from its more **southward** position of a week ago.

Cf. British:
The **forward** flank moved **towards** the north, **backwards** from its more **southward** position of a week ago.

---

amount, number; much, many

A *number* of items can be counted; there are *many* of them.
An *amount* is measured differently, as by weight; much can be said about such amounts.

- This article's analysis relies on a large ~~amount~~ → **number** of primary sources.
- Use this checkout line if you have 15 items or **fewer**.
- I don't have **much** change; how **many** quarters does the meter take for an hour of parking?

less, fewer

Fewer modifies countable nouns; *less* modifies mass or noncount nouns. Plural things are generally countable; one would have *fewer*, not *less* of them.

- There seems to be **less change** in the jar now. Yesterday it had seventy quarters; now it has ten **quarters fewer**.

See I. GRAMMAR: Grammar Charts; GARNER, MODERN LEGAL USAGE 231 (count nouns and mass nouns).

fractions & percentages

A portion of something is considered a count noun or a noncount noun, depending on what is being measured.

- One fifth of the students **are** non-Caucasian.
- Twenty percent of the chocolate **is** yours.

---

as *or* since → because *or* for

When causation is the intended meaning, a word whose meaning might initially be ambiguous (*as*, *since*) should be avoided, particularly when that word and the subordinate clause it initiates begin the sentence, so the context is not yet clear.

~~Since~~ / As → **Because** the Renaissance followed a period of cultural somnolence, some think of it as the inception of western civilization as we know it.

Some members of the gay community expect genetics research on homosexuality to advance gay rights, ~~as~~ → **for** courts view homosexuality as behavioral and not immutable like race and sex....[2]

For *as* v. *like*, see **like, as**, below.	~~Since / As~~ → **Because** courts view homosexuality as behavioral and not immutable like race and sex…, some members of the gay community expect genetics research on homosexuality to advance gay rights.
The [case name] court … **Many judges** dislike the courts on which they sit to be referred to by the name of a case the court has decided.	**Disfavored:** The *Heller* Court held that the D.C. handgun ban violated the Second Amendment. **Preferred:** In *Heller*, the Court held that the D.C. handgun ban violated the Second Amendment.
either, neither counterpoise two elements, not more. **Exception:** *Nor* may be repeated, preceding additional elements, for emphasis.	• Your objection is **neither** here **nor** there. • **Neither** rain **nor** heat **nor** gloom of night stays these couriers from the swift completion of their appointed rounds.[3]
farther, further **(a)** *Farther* refers to physical distances; *further*, to figurative ones. **(b)** If the distance seems to be both figurative and physical, let context dictate the choice.	**(a)** • She ran **farther** than he had; we ran **farthest** of all. • On **further** reflection, we realized we had mistakenly turned right. **(b)** ~~Further~~ → **Farther** down the spectrum are studies of complex errant behavior. *"Spectrum," though used here figuratively, is an actual physical object; "farther" is the better choice.*
find, hold • A judge (or court) **finds** facts — the particulars. "Finding" is the province of lower courts, not, ordinarily, of appellate courts. • What a court (or judge) **holds** answers the issue. It is stated as a general principle. • If a judge or court states such a principle that is part of the analysis but that does not directly answer the issue, the judge **concluded**, **determined**, **stated**, etc.	• The trial judge **found** that the mayor's proclamation had been stated publicly. • Although state appellate courts have ~~found~~ **[held]** **[concluded]** **[determined]** that the Florida voucher program does not run afoul of other constitutional provisions, a county district court ~~found~~ **concluded** that it violates the provision forbidding indirect aid to religious institutions.[4]

| **impact (n)** = a forceful striking of one body against another; a significant effect | The **impact** of the bus on our bumper **affect**ed us all adversely and **effect**ed a sorry dent on my "If You Can Read This, You're Too Close" bumper sticker. |

---

impact (vt, vi)

Yes, **impact** is also a verb. (*See* WEBSTER'S.) But it should not be used to mean **(i)** "affect" or "influence" or **(ii)** in place of another word that more precisely denotes the action being described.

(i) The accident ~~impacted on~~ [affected] our peace of mind grievously.

(ii) The bus ~~impacted~~ [smashed] our bumper.

---

imply, infer

imply = to express indirectly (WEBSTER'S)

Cf. a "doctrinally imposed fact," as a court would, in the exercise of its equitable powers, imply a condition or a remedy

See GARNER, MODERN LEGAL USAGE 423–25.

infer = to deduce; to arrive at a point by following a chain of reasoning (WEBSTER'S)

• A citation introduced by *see* often requires an explanation in parenthesis as to what point the reader may **infer** from consulting the cited source; the point is not stated directly, but can be deduced from what *is* stated.

• Rather than state that point directly, the source itself **implies** or suggests it; it is a point one can read "between the lines."

---

important, importantly

• *Important*, an adjective, modifies nouns.

• *Importantly*, an adverb, modifies verbs, adjectives, phrases, or entire clauses.

• *First, firstly,* etc., can likewise be used either as adjectives or adverbs. When enumerating, though, the simpler, adjective form is preferred.

Cf. thus, thusly, below

• Most **important** was the organization's → [agreement] to endorse a set of uniform standards.

• Most **importantly**, → [the organization agreed to endorse a set of uniform standards].

• **First,** the organization agreed to endorse a uniform set of standards.

---

like, as

• *Like* compares nouns or noun phrases.

• *As* compares verbal actions or states.

NB: *As* compares actions even when the second verb or clause is elided.

• ~~Like~~ As → [in the United States], technical expertise at the international level resides primarily in the private sector.[5]

• Like → [technical expertise] at the international level, such expertise at the local level resides primarily in the private sector.

NB: Acronyms are treated **as** proper nouns [**are treated**] and take no article.

Cf. Acronyms are **like** proper nouns in that they take no article.

---

not ... but ...

not only ... but [also] ...

If one element of a parallel idiom like this is used, both must be used (though the *also* is optional).

For punctuation of such idioms, see II. PUNCTUATION: Commas — Contrasted Elements.

Including in the negotiation the liberalization of agricultural trade was a *sine qua non* **not only** for the major agricultural exporters such as the United States and the Cairns Group led by Australia **but also** for many developing countries.[6]

Cf. Including in the negotiation the liberalization of agricultural trade was a *sine qua non* for the major agricultural exporters such as the United States and the Cairns Group led by Australia ~~but also~~ → **and** for many developing countries, **as well**.

---

on the one hand, ... on the other hand, ...

It is **permissible** to have one hand and not the other.

Although lawyers should want to satisfy this responsibility **on the one hand** to avoid liability, they should want to do so as well to safeguard their reputations and integrity.

---

question, ask, query

To question can mean more than *to ask*; it includes "to subject to analysis" or "interrogate closely" (WEBSTER'S), whereas *to ask* means, more simply, to pose a question.

Query (n.) is a question, inquiry, or doubt;

to query (vt) is to question or inquire, often wishing more authoritative information or to resolve a doubt.

• The moderator **questioned** why the research had focused on one particular ethnic group and not on another; a panel participant **asked** when the group would break for lunch.

Either "ask" or "question" would be correct in the first clause of this example, though the use of "question" for issues that evidently trouble the asker is more appropriate; "ask" is the better choice when the asker is probing more for an answer than for an explanation.

• **Query** the author whether this pun is intended.

simplistic v. simple

Simplistic does not mean plain and straightforward (*simple*), but overly simple — the result of having "reduced a problem to a false simplicity by ignoring complicating factors." WEBSTER'S 1162.

Under Judge Sack's simplistic logic simple negligence is a more demanding test than constitutional malice![7]

---

that, which

(a) Use *that* to introduce a **defining** clause, one essential to understanding the sentence.

(b) Use *which* to introduce a **nondefining** clause — one whose information is not essential to understanding which noun is meant, information that is basically parenthetical.

See H.W. FOWLER, MODERN ENGLISH USAGE 626; GARNER, MODERN LEGAL USAGE 765–67.

For when the "that" in defining clauses can be dropped, see IV. USAGE: Usage & Verbosity, below.

(a) [G]enetics research tends to focus on discrete and insular populations **that** share a common ancestry....[8]

(b) These groups, **which** often overlap with socially constructed racial or ethnic minority groups, have proved to be a laboratory for genetics research.

---

thus, thusly

Both forms are adverbs, so adding the *–ly* is superfluous and, some would say, pretentious.

Cf. important, importantly

Thus spoke Zarathustra.

---

truth, truism

A truism is an obvious truth.

[J]udicial notice applies to self-evident truths that no reasonable person could question, truisms that approach platitudes or banalities.[9]

---

utilize v. use

To utilize something means more than simply to use it; it means to put to practical use.

This bucket used to catch drips can be utilized as a stepstool when you get around to patching the ceiling.

where

(a) Use as a locative for a geographical or abstract place

or

(b) in mathematical legends or definitions.

(a) [He] was so obsessively pro-slavery that he refused … even to enter **any state where** slavery had been abolished.[10]

(a) **Where** personal liberty ends and society's constraints begin is not easy to pin down.

(a) Even at this end of **the sociological spectrum** however, **where** the relationship between personal liberty and social constraint is most strained …

(b) where χ is the distance between the county seat and the farthest point of the county's jurisdictional boundary

---

Where **should not be used in lieu of** *when, whenever,* **or** *whereas* **to indicate particular facts, circumstances, or conditions. Such use is common in speech and informal writing, but it is inappropriate for the formal style of academic writing.**

See generally GARNER, MODERN LEGAL USAGE 928–29.

• **Where** [→ **When**] errors are asserted a trial judge of excellent repute will be given the benefit of every doubt. Even **when** he has erred, he will be treated as though he made an understandable mistake…. [11]

• It is often unclear in which global decisionmaking arrangements one could or should establish participatory rights, or which actions should be reviewable [~~where~~] **when,** [*or whenever*] binding instruments and decisions are absent.[12]

• [~~Where~~] → [W]**hereas** the Massachusetts law imposes explicit limitations on the use of the bio-identification records, the Nevada statute makes no mention of any allowed uses.[13]

Where **should not be used in lieu of** *in which* **or** *for which,* **as when referring to a case.**

• It applies only [**to cases** ~~where~~] → [**in which**] the consumer's claim is based on statutory rights, not [~~where~~] → **when** it is based on nonstatutory rights, such as common-law contract or tort duties.[14]

• **When the court has turned to foreign materials in major cases, it has usually been in areas of law** ~~**where**~~ [**in which**] U.S. sources had yet to exist.[15]

• Congress and surrogate administrative agencies followed Roosevelt's lead and regulated corporations through other bodies of law, ~~where~~ [**in which**] federal authority was more firm.[16]

• The "injury in fact" prong is the element ~~where~~ most plaintiffs fail to achieve standing. →
• The "injury in fact" prong is the element most plaintiffs seeking standing fail to prove.

Exception: *Where* is permissible **for the sake of brevity** when referring to a situation or circumstance.

Exception:
~~Under circumstances in which~~ → [**Where**] federal regulation of business was once minimal, now it is extensive.

Where **should not be used in lieu of** *whenever* to refer to repeated or repeatable situations or circumstances.

I recommend that ~~in every situation where~~ [**whenever**] a court faces a choice between domestic law and international law, it should choose the latter.

Where **should not be used in lieu of** *whereby* (meaning *by which*) or *wherein* (meaning *in which*)

One way of understanding the offense is in terms of the separation of powers[,] [**whereby**] the judiciary has the role of determining in an open trial both guilt and appropriate punishment.[17]

The notion that private actors are the subjects of global regulation is also evident in much of the regulatory governance accomplished through networks, **wherein** the national regulatory officials perform both an international-level … and a domestic-level role….[18]

which, that

Use *which* as the relative pronoun introducing nondefining clauses (whose information is not essential to understanding what noun is referred to) and *that* as the relative pronoun introducing defining clauses. A *which* clause is set off by commas; a *that* clause is not.

See II. PUNCTUATION: Commas — Commas & No Commas.

• These groups, **which** often overlap with socially constructed racial or ethnic minority groups, have proved to be a laboratory for genetics research.
• The groups **that** overlap most with socially constructed racial or ethnic minority groups have proved to be laboratories for genetics research.

of which, for which

When two (or more) relative-pronoun clauses follow **and define** a noun, both should be "*that*" **unless** the second clause **follows a preposition**: then *which* is used in lieu of *that*.

For parallel defining phrases uncomplicated by the above construction, use *that* for both.

• The response **that** the candidate ultimately gave and **in which** he rationalized his ignorance of the facts satisfied no one.

Cf. The response **that** the candidate ultimately gave and **that** satisfied no one was no more than a rationalization of his ignorance of the facts.

while, although, whereas

(a) Avoid using **while** (meaning **although**) to initiate a subordinate clause preceding the main clause. Rather, use **although** or **whereas** or another equivalent word or construction to avoid starting the reader off in the wrong direction. When, on the other hand, **while** means "at the same time," it can unambiguously initiate the subordinate clause wherever it is situated.

(b) When the subordinate phrase or clause introduced by **while** follows the main clause, the potential for confusion tends not to arise. Nevertheless, **while** is often less precise than an alternative.

(a) [~~While~~] **Although** genes may constrain or influence behavior, they do so only in concert with each other and with the environment that is both internal and external to the organism carrying the genes.[19]

(a) **While** [= **at the same time that**] they were concerned about their son's growing symptoms of alcoholism, they were also wary of the study's potential impact on their family.[20]

(b) The results demonstrated that the high activity form of the gene did not manifest in violent propensities even if the men had been mistreated as boys, **while** [→ **whereas**] those with the low-active form of the gene who had been mistreated committed four times as many rapes, assaults, and robberies as the average.[21]

(b) Most evidence for a genetic basis of antisocial behavior stems from classical studies estimating the global effects of genes and environment, [~~while~~ →] **yet** several molecular studies are beginning to emerge identifying specific genetic associations.[22]

Word Choice: Auxiliary Verbs
(**can, could, do, may, might,** must, need, ought, shall, should)

These verbs may have other meanings, but they have certain denotations or connotations when used as auxiliaries. *See also* I. GRAMMAR: Verbs — Subjunctive Mood.

• **Can** denotes ability.	• **Can** you dance? Yes, I **can.**
• Followed by an explicit or implicit verb, its past form, **could,** expresses the subjunctive mood and connotes condition.	• I would dance, if I **could.**

Do in a parallel construction can substitute for the verb.	Do you dance? Yes, I **do** [dance].

May can denote or express

(a) permission,

(b) wish, or

(c) purpose, contingency, expectation (e.g., it is possible that, possibly will).

Followed by an explicit or implicit verb, its subjunctive form, **might,** *connotes greater uncertainty* than the indicative "may," including

(d) wish, probability, possibility, or

(e) a condition contrary to fact.

(f) The choice of the indicative or subjunctive mood for the remainder of the verb phrase can enhance this difference. To give the reader a clear message as to the writer's certainty or doubt, both verbs should be in the same mood.

(a) You may dance, if you wish.

(b) May it rain soon!

(c) I may dance later.

(c) The department itself **may** have sanctioned the release of the tapes.

(d) I might dance later.

(d), (c) Thus, from the perspective of smaller developing countries, global regulatory institutions including the WTO, IMF, World Bank, and U.N. Security Council **might** already appear to be "administering" them at the bidding of the industrialized countries, which are generally subject to far less intrusive external regulation. Confronting these issues in administrative terms **may** highlight the need to devise strategies for remedying unfairness associated with such inequalities.[23]

(e) It might have sprinkled, but it poured.

(f) **It may be** *(indicative)* that implementing these proposals simply **increases** *(indicative)* the quantity of messages without adding any new ideas.[24]

Cf.

It might be *(subjunctive)* that implementing these proposals **would increase** *(subjunctive)* the quantity of messages without adding any new ideas.

May have v. might have: Perhaps because the meaning of "may" in its past indicative form (may have) is sometimes ambiguous, some editors recommend using "might" to express the past of "may," whatever its meaning in the indicative mood. *See* WEBSTER'S DICTIONARY OF ENGLISH USAGE 627.

It might have sprinkled, but it poured.
  (I.e., It could have merely sprinkled, but…)

But these forms are not synonymous, as this example illustrates. →

Cf. It may have sprinkled, but we stayed dry.
  (I.e., It sprinkled, but…)

"May" meaning "shall, must," acknowledged by WEBSTER'S as being "used in law [when] the sense, purpose or policy requires this interpretation" **should not be so used** in law or elsewhere. When courts have contorted the definition of "may" to mean "must," they were legislating.

"Must" denotes obligation or necessity.

· **Must** we dance all night?

· We **must.**

"Need" denotes necessity or obligation.

· You **need** not dance, if you're not inclined.

· I **need** to leave.

"Ought" denotes duty, obligation, or expectation. Retain the "to" of the infinitive that follows.

· You **ought to dance.**

· We **ought to be** home by now.

"Shall" can express duty or compulsion, or it can express expectation. Its use to express a mandate has therefore provoked debate; some have suggested that "must" be substituted.

Whether interpreted as expectation or mandate, though, "shall" plainly means that the actor has no choice: the action will occur.

See WEBSTER'S 1143.

· The mayor **shall** resign the term at the end of the calendar year. *(mandate? expectation?)*

· Judgment **shall** be entered in accordance with this court's determination. *(mandate)*

· We **shall** overcome someday. *(expectation)*

"Should," the past tense of **shall,** is the form **shall** takes in the subjunctive mood and denotes **(a)** condition, **(b)** duty or obligation, **(c)** expectation or probability, or is used to **(d)** soften a direct statement.	**(a)** If ever I **should** leave you, it would not be in summer. **(a)** I enclose my article, **should** you care to read it (i.e., if you should care to read it). **(b)** I **should** leave now. **(c)** It **should** be fine tomorrow. **(d)** You **should** proofread this one more time.
"Will" connotes future; its past form, **"would,"** the form **"will"** takes in the subjunctive mood, connotes condition.	• You **will** dance again, one of these days. • I **would** dance if I could.

Usage & Verbosity

"That," in general: minimize its use unless doing so results in ambiguity. **(a)** The *that* initiating a defining clause can often be dropped or substituted by (i) a participle — the verb in its adjective form or (ii) an adjective phrase. **(b)** The *that* should not be dropped if misreading might result, as when the *that* clause is the direct object of the preceding verb. This is especially likely if the verb, like *assume, hold, determine, decide,* can be read more than one way. **Verbs for which "that" can usually be elided:** believe, confess, consider, declare, grant, hear, know, perceive, presume propose, say, see, suppose, think, understand.	**(a)** The greatest competitive advantage [~~that~~] local merchants enjoy … **(i)** [G]enetics research tends to focus on discrete and insular populations [~~that share~~] → **sharing** a common ancestry….[25] **(ii)** [G]enes may … influence behavior … in concert with each other and with the environment [~~that is~~] **both internal and external to the organism** that carries the genes.[26] **(b)** • This paper states **that** the answer is for entrants to be supported by community institutions. **Cf.** This paper states the answer…. • The Court held **that** a monument of the Ten Commandments is not unconstitutional if displayed beside secular, historical monuments. **Cf.** The Court held a monument….

Verbs for which "that" is "usual":

agree, announce, argue, assume, aver, calculate, conceive, contend, hold, indicate, learn, maintain, observe, reckon, remark, state, suggest.

H.W. Fowler, Modern English Usage 624.

(c) Ambiguity is unlikely if the direct object is a pronoun in the nominative case.

(c)
- The judge **found they** had appeared before her in the past.
- I **knew he** was a leading scholar.

More than one *that* clause: Even if an initial *that* introducing a clause can be eliminated, if the sentence has a second, it must have the first.

The greatest competitive advantage **that** local merchants enjoy and **that** most concerns warehouse mailorder outfits is the ability to serve the consumer shopping on a whim.

Too many indispensable *thats*?

Revise.

Rather, all it requires is **that** the tensions created by such a law are understood as tensions **that** are internal to legal order, tensions **that** must be resolved in order for **that** legal order to sustain its claim to be such — an order constituted by law.[27]

Revised:
Rather, all it requires is **for** the tensions created by such a law **to be** understood as tensions internal to legal order, tensions **that** must be resolved in order for **that** legal order to sustain its claim to be such — an order constituted by law.

The fact that and its even lengthier permutations (*because of the fact that*, *despite the fact that*) are almost always dispensable,

either

(a) by substituting *that*, alone,

or

(a) ~~The fact that~~ [That] many state and local governments have amended their employment discrimination laws to add protection for gay and lesbian employees has made no impression on Congress.

(b) by revising the sentence.

(b) ~~[D]espite the fact that~~ [**Although**] many state and local governments have amended their employment discrimination laws to add protection for gay and lesbian employees, Congress has remained intransigent.

(b) ~~But the fact that~~ [**That**] the Y chromosome is strongly correlated with crime is not touted as a rationale to change social policy, perhaps in part because most policymakers are men.[28]

(b) But the strong correlation of the Y chromosome with crime is not touted as a rationale to change social policy....

The fact that: *exception for style*

when the author wishes to emphasize that the conditions or circumstances are, in fact, fact.

The fact that between three and five million poor children die every year of diarrhea that can be prevented with an oral rehydration formula costing eight cents per dose has not inspired a movement to rebuke the United States government and American companies.[29]

Whether

- Do not use **"as to whether"** or **" ... of whether"**

- usually do not use **"whether or not"** (because "or not" is often, but not always, implied).

- question ~~as to~~ whether

- issue ~~of~~ whether

- decision ~~as to~~ whether

- determination ~~as to~~ whether

Exception: whether or not—
In the same way, the Security Council's delegation of power to the Committee—and the Committee's subsequent exercise of authority—lacked legal authority, **whether or not** one accepts that the Security Council is entitled to legislate.[30]

Most domestic systems of administrative law address the issue of executive branch officers or administrative agencies (**whether** politically independent **or not**)....[31]

Deciding to do → just **do** it.	• Last October the government decided to dismiss its case against the detainee.
	• Last October the government dismissed its case against the detainee.
Exception for style: the decision was perhaps more important than the getting it done.	*Exception:* Last October, after months of indecision, the government decided at last to dismiss its case against the detainee.
It/There is, there are … that	• **There is** surprisingly little biological research **that** has been done on sex offenders.
Revise to eliminate these word-wasters.	• Surprisingly little biological research has been done on sex offenders.[32]
	• Despite their signing the treaty, **there were** substantial differences of opinion among the signatories. →
	• Despite their signing the treaty, the signatories harbored substantial differences of opinion.
Exception for style: The *there is / was …* construction throws the emphatic weight of the sentence to its end.	*Exception:* There was talk that AIDS was a plague sent against the homosexuals by a wrathful God.[33]
For overreliance on the empty verb "to be," see IV. USAGE & STYLE — Style: Ineffectiveness (Passive Voice), below.	

Style: Effectiveness & Emphasis

It is ordinarily the province of the author, not the editor, to enhance an article's style. Nonetheless, modest and clearly explained suggestions for more effective phrasing or structure will likely be appreciated. Such effective expression follows these principles:

Words

Effective word choice — not sesquipedalian, flashy ones, but fresh ones, vivid ones, precise ones.	After all, for most innovations and inventions one needs hardware, capital investment, and large-scale, real-world data collection — *stuff*, in its infinite recalcitrance and facticity. Maybe the open-source model has solved the individual incentives problem, but that's not the *only* problem.[34]
Judiciously used italics →	

Effective Modifier Placement

Place the modifier as close to the word or phrase modified as possible, so long as ambiguity is avoided.

Whether the modifier should precede or follow the word or phrase modified depends on the syntax (how the sentence parts are put together) and on the modifier. Here, because "however" is parenthetical and causes the voice to drop, its placement after the word modified emphasizes the word that precedes it.

The court, however, failed to provide any guidelines for determining what would constitute prohibitive expense.

Here, the placement of "however" emphasizes the court, rather than the court's failure.

Cf.
The court failed, however, to provide any guidelines for determining what would constitute prohibitive expense.

Cf. *When the modifier is placed after "guidelines," the emphasis is on the absent guidelines, rather than on the court's failure:*
The court failed to provide any guidelines, however, for determining what would constitute prohibitive expense.

***However* modifying entire sentence:**

A sentence **may** begin with *however*, but this is rarely the most effective place for it or the most effective word choice under the circumstances.

Consumers have proved to be successful in many arbitration cases. However, → **But** their success may be at some cost.

OR

Their success, **however,** may be at some cost.

However should never end a sentence because transition words that point backward should come early in the sentence and because the end of the sentence should be reserved for its most important information.

Ineffective:

[C]onsumers have prevailed in several reported cases. Winning may require substantial expertise and resources, **however.**

Effective:

• [C]onsumers have prevailed in several reported cases. Winning, **however,** may require substantial expertise and resources.[35]

• [C]onsumers have prevailed in several reported cases. **Yet** winning may require substantial expertise and resources.

Limiting or emphasizing modifiers are most effectively placed just in front of the word or phrase they limit.	• **Only** → I wear Prada. *(I.e., no one else does, including the devil.)*
	• I **only** → wear Prada. *(I.e., e.g., I don't sell it.)*
	• I wear **only** → Prada. *(I.e., I wear no other designer.)*
	• I wear Prada, ← **only**. *(In this position, because **only** comes last, it gets the emphasis, but the placement introduces some ambiguity as to what, exactly, is limited.)*
Avoid separating the subject from its verb.	• Discussions of behavioral genetics and crime **markedly** tend to focus on violent behaviors.[36] → • Discussions of behavioral genetics and crime tend to focus **markedly** on violent behaviors.
Where to split the verb phrase: Many grammarians consider the most effective placement of an adverb to be immediately after the first auxiliary verb. *E.g.,* BRYAN GARNER, THE RED-BOOK 151. But this preference is subject to what the writer wishes to emphasize. The emphasis tends to fall on the word ending the verb phrase. If emphasis is important to the writer, then the adverb should immediately precede that word (unless the adverb comes last, in which case it gets the emphasis).	• They **unfairly** have been segregated from mainstream society and excluded from the political process.[37] *Adverb undesirably intrudes between subject and verb.* → They **have unfairly been segregated** from mainstream society and excluded from the political process. ***Cf.*** They have been **unfairly** segregated from mainstream society and excluded from the political process. *Emphasis falls on "segregated."* OR: • They have been segregated **unfairly** from mainstream society and excluded from the political process. *Emphasis falls on "unfairly."* *"Unfairly" is better placed here than at the tail end of the phrase, "They have been segregated from mainstream society unfairly," only because the farther the adverb gets from the verb it modifies, the less punch it delivers.*
Splitting infinitive phrases is likewise acceptable.	The President intends **to generously expand** the number of soldiers in the field.

Modifier placement and parallelism Regardless of where the modifier is placed, its placement should be the same in parallel phrases.	In constitutional law, racial and ethnic minority groups are "discrete" in that **they can generally be identified** by a distinct and often immutable trait, and they are "insular" because **they have historically been segregated** from mainstream society and excluded from the political process.[38]

Effective Sentences

Proximity of subject and verb When a sentence is in the active voice, keeping the subject as close to the verb as possible gives the sentence a focal point, as well as immediacy and punch.	*Active:* **The Court failed** to provide any guidelines for determining what would constitute prohibitive expense.
Exception: When the sentence is in the passive voice, the subject (the actor) is less important (and thus often absent) than the object (the acted upon), so this rule does not apply. *See* Style: Ineffectiveness — Passive Voice.	*Exception — Passive voice:* Guidelines for determining what would constitute prohibited expense were not provided.
Sentences build from context to climax. The subject and verb, the focal point of a sentence (its "core"), may be preceded by (or incorporate) **context** orienting the reader. The end of the sentence is its **climax**, a.k.a. its "stress" position. *See* GEORGE GOPEN, THE SENSE OF STRUCTURE 37 (2004); JOSEPH KIMBLE, LIFTING THE FOG OF LEGALESE 71 (2006); JOSEPH WILLIAMS, STYLE: TEN LESSONS IN CLARITY AND GRACE 65 (3d ed. 1989).	In the United States [*context*], the widespread impression was that the problem had been solved [*climax*]. According to newspapers and television [*context*], there had been two problems [*climax*]: high prices and the suit that kept the South African government from doing something about them [*appositive extending climax*]. These [*context*] fit the classic American picture of an abuse [*climax*]: an aberration in a broader pattern in which everything is more or less okay [*appositive extending climax*]. Someone is doing something wrong [*context*: evokes "an aberration"], and once the wrongdoer is stopped, things will right themselves [*climax*].[39]

Emphatic prose and effective transitions from sentence to sentence or from paragraph to paragraph often rely on these patterns.

Things have failed to right themselves. [*context "things" & transition via structure parallel to that in the last sentence above*][40]

Varied sentence length

The sentences in the first paragraph of this example go from 14 words to 26 to 23 to 15. The effect of the paragraph is a modest rise and fall. Although each sentence models context and climax, the paragraph itself is context, which ends in a pseudo-climax undone almost immediately by the topic sentence of the next paragraph.

The brevity of the quite short final sentence (6 words) snaps the reader to attention.

In the United States, the widespread impression was that the problem had been solved. According to newspapers and television, there had been two problems: high prices and the suit that kept the South African government from doing something about them. These fit the classic American picture of an abuse: an aberration in a broader pattern in which everything is more or less okay. Someone is doing something wrong, and once the wrongdoer is stopped, things will right themselves.

Things have failed to right themselves.[41]

Repetition (of key words, phrases, sounds, constructions) and, more generally, parallel structure makes writing more cohesive and can provide a rhythm that draws the reader into the prose.

Someone is doing something wrong, and once the wrongdoer is stopped, **things will right themselves.** **Things have failed to right themselves.**[42]

In bloody-minded diasporas and nationalisms, the memory of wounds tells people **who they are, who is their brother,** and **whom they ought to hate.**[43]

The **more divergent the interests are** among state parties to the institution, **the more decisionmaking is** relegated to the treaty bodies; and **the more checks and balances there are** between competing bodies within the institution, **the more elaborate is** the administrative law that develops.[44]

Rhetorical Questions

Rhetorical questions are questions posed by the writer to pique the reader's interest, not to provoke an answer.

(a) They can be used as **transitions** at the end or beginning of a section to set up the discussion that will follow.

(b) They can be used to make a **substantive** point. The question, as posed, answers itself. Unless the question is actually answered (as in this example), this use can lead to the reader's confusion. Stating the point directly, outright, rather than interrogatively will be more clear unless the context of the question makes the answer unmistakable.

(a) Should personal norms ever substitute for societal norms as a behavioral rubric? The question is not new, though it is rarely discussed seriously.

(b) Whether the internet has its own legal order depends, then, on whether we recognize it as one. Is this recognition in the sense of conflict of laws? Is it the acknowledgment that the normative order of the internet can be the "applicable law" in a choice of law process, that "decisions" of the internet should be enforced by state courts? Although they do not say so explicitly, Johnson and Post argue in this direction when they ask the state to grant comity to the normative order of the internet.[45]

Rhetorical questions within a sentence: When the question does not stand on its own, it may (but need not) be preceded by a comma or a colon or be enclosed in em-dashes.

The rhetorical question need not begin with a capital letter, but it may; and it ought to if (1) the question is formally introduced and follows a colon, (2) the question is lengthy, or (3) it has internal punctuation (to signal clearly to the reader that a question is being introduced).

- Not content with merely good science, decision-makers and the public are also asking, and advisedly so, What is science good for, and is it good enough to serve those purposes?[46]

- Yet modern societies' increasing dependence on science has proceeded hand in hand with developments that disable most citizens, even the most technically expert, from effectively addressing the larger set of questions: Is it good science; what is it good for; … is it good enough?[47]

- In the case of public, or policy-relevant, science, the question, How transparent should science be? thus entails an automatic corollary: To whom should it be transparent?[48]

Style: Ineffectiveness

Anthropomorphism Human traits should not be ascribed to nonhuman entities.	Criminal law is now particularly interested in behavioral conditions that contribute to violence. → **Those who study and work in** criminal law are now particularly interested in behavioral conditions that contribute to violence.
Passive voice: phrasing a sentence by putting the verb's object first so the subject is not acting but acted upon, not active but passive. The verb phrase is a form of *to be* plus the verb's past participle. The effect renders the actor invisible **(a)** or less important by way of being suspended from a preposition **(b)**. The latter is unnecessarily wordy; the former is undesirable *unless* the writer intends to hide the actor or to stress the action or its effect, rather than the actor.	**(a)** The glass was broken. **(b)** The glass was broken by Martha.
***Cf.* Active voice**: phrasing a sentence so the actor is its subject.	***Cf.*** Martha broke the glass.
***Stylistic exception* for passive voice:** when the author intends to **(a)** hide the actor or **(b)** stress the action or its object. *See also* IV: USAGE & STYLE: Person, below.	**(a)** Mistakes were made. **(b)** Congress has been unimpressed that many state and local governments have amended their employment discrimination laws to add protection for gay and lesbian employees. *(active voice)* ***Cf.*** That many state and local governments have amended their employment discrimination laws to add protection for gay and lesbian employees has made no impression on Congress. *(passive voice)* *The latter passage not only puts the most important point in the climax position, but the passive voice mirrors the passivity of Congress.*

(b) Arguably, the same series of missteps is now being urged by network providers (the telcos, cablecos, and wirelesscos) in the network[-]neutrality debate.[49] *(passive voice)*
The focal point of the sentence is on the subject, the series of missteps.

Cf. Arguably, network providers (the telcos, cablecos, and wirelesscos) are urging the same series of missteps in the network-neutrality debate. *(active voice)*
Here, the focal point is "network providers";"missteps" is buried.

Style: Person

In expository articles and in any formal legal document, the objective is to discuss a topic other than the author, so first person should be avoided. The presence of the writer can compete with her subject (which even the writer would agree is more important for the article's purposes than she is). The writer's presence may be called for (she might think) when she is stating her opinion; yet it is obvious that any opinion stated in the article is hers because she is its author. (Such self-reference is arguably more tolerable in the introduction, where the reader might expect to see it (but not miss its absence); or in footnotes, which, should the reader choose to read them, have by their very nature already distracted him; or in the conclusion, by which time the spell of an exposition standing on its own may be broken, anyway.)

Exception: When the author is herself the subject, as when she is recounting a personal experience or describing her role in the development of a literature or the limited scope of her analysis, then first person may be appropriate.

Second person is little better. "You," like "I," has the effect of intruding between the subject and the reader's consciousness. Moreover, addressing the reader smacks of the eighteenth-century omniscient (and officious) narrator, whose directives can give more umbrage than direction to the reader.

First person plural exception for style: "We," when it signifies the writer and the reader or society in general (and not, for example, coauthors), is acceptable when not overused. The intent and effect is to include the reader in the problem or inquiry being addressed.

Conventions versus style. Some writers sport an informal style whereby they intend to put the reader at ease, to chat their way into his consciousness, to figuratively take his elbow and so guide him through the text. The use of first and second person is often liberally used by such writers.

(Note to editors: Such authors dislike editorial meddling, and if their writing communicates effectively otherwise, the editor would be wise to point out that the use of first and second person is discouraged by more formal journal convention, but, if resisted, to let it go.)

In formal legal documents — briefs, memoranda of law — first and second person simply have no place.

Active voice is generally preferred to passive, but **passive voice** is one means of avoiding use of the first person.

Passive voice can also be a stylistic choice, focusing the sentence on a subject that is not the agent. *See* IV. USAGE & STYLE: Ineffectiveness (Passive Voice), above.

- **Active**, undesirable: In part II of this article, I discuss and critique …

- **Active**, but undesirably anthropomorphic *(because the article does not discuss or critique (or argue); rather, it is the means for the author to do so)*:

  Part II of this article discusses and critiques the courts' use of future-dangerousness predictions in sentencing and post-sentence commitment proceedings for capital murderers and sex offenders and in community notification requirements for sex offenders.[50]

  See also V. USAGE & STYLE: Ineffectiveness (Anthropomorphism), above.

- **Passive, logical, and more effective** *because the subject of the article is more prominent than in the above example; that the treatment will be at the hands of the author is obvious and need not be stated. The author's attitude toward courts is implicit but clear in the second sentence:*

  In part II of this article, the courts' use of future-dangerousness predictions is discussed and critiqued. Courts not only rely on such predictors in sentencing and post-sentence commitment proceedings for capital murderers and sex offenders, but they permit its even more dubious use in community notification requirements for sex offenders.

- **Active, logical, and most effective** *because, although the more interesting verbs "discuss" and "critique" have been nominalized, the first sentence ends with what is most important to the author — the courts' use of these predictions.*

  Part II of this article includes a discussion and critique of the courts' use of future-dangerousness predictions. Courts not only rely on such predictors in sentencing and post-sentence commitment proceedings for capital murderers and sex offenders, but they permit its even more dubious use in community notification requirements for sex offenders.

Style: Paragraph Structure — Topic & Transition Sentences

In legal documents such as office memoranda and briefs, each paragraph begins with a **topic sentence** stating the paragraph's topic, which is then developed through detail, documentation, and discussion. The same goes for readable scholarly writing, whether expository or argumentative. A paragraph may also (or, rarely, alternatively — *see* **acceptable alternatives below)** include a **transition sentence** at the beginning or end, which overtly links the paragraph to the preceding paragraph. Or, more nuanced **transitional signals** may be part of the topic sentence itself.

The underlined topic sentences in the examples below not only state the paragraph's topic, but give it a thematic focus; repeating the thematic phrase helps the two paragraphs cohere. The bracketed *Economic as well as credential incentives* in the highlighted topic sentence in ¶ 2 is a clear transition from the preceding paragraph [excluded here], whose topic was scholarly incentives to withhold data. In ¶ 3, the repetition of the overarching topic (incentives) and the **transitional signal** *also* (like *as well as* in ¶ 2) likewise link the paragraphs' topics.

¶ 1   [Scholarly incentives to withhold data: to enhance credentials]

¶ 2   [Economic **as well as** credential incentives] affect a researcher's interest in sharing unpublished data. All scientific researchers without unlimited personal wealth need funding to conduct research and will therefore inevitably be conscious of where the next grant or contract is coming from. Thus, even academic researchers are likely at least to think about the effect on their current or future sources of funding when determining whether, when, and how to disclose their results and the data underlying them.

¶ 3   Economic incentives **also** affect the behavior of nonprofit professional associations. The American Chemical Society (ACS) recently secured congressional assistance in protecting its fee-based Chemical Abstracts Service (CAS) Registry — historically *the* reference database for information on the structure and property of chemicals — from possible competition by "Pub-Chem," a free database operated by the National Institutes of Health (NIH). ACS is understandably concerned that PubChem may — at taxpayer expense — replicate portions of the CAS generated at substantial expense by ACS, this example confirms that economic incentives can lead even nonprofit professional associations to take actions at least facially inconsistent with "free" science.[51]

A lengthy topic may be developed in more than one subsequent paragraph, each one initiated by a topic sentence focused on that part of the development. In the sentence below, the enumeration and repeated subject, "characteristic," initiating the topic sentences in the second and third paragraphs are **transitional signals** alluding to the larger, enveloping topic. Such clear transition signals are important in a new paragraph, as is an unmistakable reminder of the topic. Even if the same topic is further developed in a new paragraph, it should be repeated, in a shorter form, perhaps, but never represented by a mere pronoun.

Example:

¶ 1   Cardozo's equity opinions, as a body, have several marked characteristics. They are, first, unabashed in moral judgments on the parties.... [Examples and elaboration follow: 149 words.]

¶ 2   A second characteristic of Cardozo's opinions is his repeated emphasis on the power of the court of equity to require adherence to moral principles, even those requiring affirmative action on the part of someone.... [Examples and elaboration follow: 111 words.]

¶ 3   A third characteristic of Cardozo's equity opinions is his insistence on the fact-specific nature of the chancellor's decisions. [Examples and elaboration follow: 119 words.][52]

Alternative to an initial topic sentence: A narrative paragraph that introduces the topic descriptively or that establishes a tone for what follows can do so without a topic sentence. Here, the last sentence, a **transition sentence**, adeptly also states the paper's topic: peer review.

Example:

On June 29, 2001, just outside Klamath Falls, Oregon, an angry mob of farmers took actions into their own hands. Massing around the closed floodgates of a federally operated irrigation ditch, the crowd defied federal government orders, burst open the floodgate locks, and returned the flow of water to the thirsty soils of their croplands. The mob stayed put and made camp for the next few days, challenging federal officials time after time by unlocking the gates as soon as they had been closed. The crowd finally was dispersed under the stern direction of United States Marshals. The battle lines could not have been more clearly drawn. The farmers cried for relief from dry irrigation ditches and the specter of failed crops. The federal government stood firm. The gates had to stay shut and farmlands go dry in order to save endangered fish dependent on the stored waters. The following March, however, amidst the flash of news cameras and proud speeches, the Secretary of Agriculture and Secretary of the Interior quite publicly opened the very same floodgates. What made the first liberation of water an act of civil disobedience and the latter a high-profile case of wise federal governance? Improbably, the answer came from a room full of scientists and a practice called peer review.[53]

Alternative to initial topic sentence: A transition sentence may precede the topic sentence.

Example 1: The **transition sentence** is last in ¶ 1 below.

¶ 1   The draft guidance document also provides numerous examples of the types of "emerging" safety information that would be communicated under the proposal.... For example,... Likewise,... Importantly, these examples involve safety information that is valid and useful. In these examples, the ... information is "emerging" only in the sense that it is newly acquired, not in the sense that it is still under investigation.

¶ 2   One of the examples that the FDA offers, however, does involve information that is still under active investigation.[54]

Example 2: The **transition sentence**, underlined in ¶ 2 below, comes first, which works extremely well so long as the sentence that follows continues to refine the topic before the paragraph develops it. This model is helpful particularly when development of the larger topic (here, the FDA website's safety information) has become so extenuated that the reader may need to be reoriented.

¶ 1   The draft guidance document also provides numerous examples of the types of "emerging" safety information that would be communicated under the proposal.... For example, ... Likewise, ... Importantly, these examples involve safety information that is valid and useful.

¶ 2   In these examples, the website's safety information is "emerging" only in the sense that it is newly acquired, not in the sense that it is still under investigation. One of the examples that [the] FDA offers, however, does involve information that is still under active investigation. According to [the] FDA, ...[55]

Avoid transition sentences at the end of a paragraph that eclipse the next topic sentence. Having a transition sentence is by no means *de rigueur*; a paragraph may end by simply completing the exposition of its topic. It is far better for the topic sentence in the next paragraph to allude to what comes before than to have the transitional material at the end of one paragraph repeated at the beginning of the next. Why? Because the reader does not expect new information at the end of a paragraph. The reader will wonder if he missed something and may feel compelled to go back and look. The end of a paragraph should wrap things up — and perhaps hint at the next package — but not open a fresh box. In the variation below, the transition sentence steals the thunder from the following paragraph, which is left with no more than supporting detail.

¶ 1   The draft guidance document also provides numerous examples of the types of "emerging" safety information that would be communicated under the proposal.... For example, ... Likewise, ... Importantly, these examples involve safety information that is valid and useful. The information is "emerging" only in the sense that it is newly acquired, not in the sense that it is still under investigation, although [the] FDA does offer one example of the latter.

¶ 2   According to FDA, the Drug Watch website will contain "factual information about newly observed, serious adverse events," such as post-marketing reports of renal failure in elderly patients, even before a causal relationship between the adverse reaction and the drug product has been established. Recognizing that the reliability of this information is unknown, FDA proposes to accompany the information with a disclaimer along the following lines:....[56]

Here are the same paragraphs, revised to put the thunder back in the topic sentence of ¶ 2. That topic sentence is revised to put the transitional material in a subordinate clause and the topic material in the main clause (with the new topic placed in the climax position) to signal even more clearly what will be developed subsequently:

¶ 1   The draft guidance document also provides numerous examples of the types of "emerging" safety information that would be communicated under the proposal.... For example, ... Likewise, ... Importantly, these examples involve safety information that is valid and useful.

¶ 2   <u>Although the safety information in the draft guidance document is "emerging" only in the sense that it is newly acquired, [the] FDA offers one example of "emerging" information as data still under investigation.</u> According to [the] FDA, the Drug Watch website will contain "factual information about newly observed, serious adverse events," such as post-marketing reports of renal failure in elderly patients, even before a causal relationship between the adverse reaction and the drug product has been established. Recognizing that the reliability of this information is unknown, [the] FDA proposes to accompany the information with a disclaimer along the following lines:....[57]

V

Conventions
Abbreviations, Numbers, Dates, Symbols, Capitalization, Italics, Lists, Spelling, URLs, & Interviews

The conventions listed here are included as prompts to the writer and editor to decide how to treat such matters — whether to follow those listed or to pencil in preferences. It matters less what the writer or editor chooses than that the choice be consistently applied: such details should never distract from the *sense* of what is being written.

Abbreviations

Words & Common Expressions: spell out or abbreviate?

In text, spell out contractions and these abbreviations:

i.e. → that is,
e.g. → for example
etc. → et cetera, and so forth …
et seq. → et sequitur
his/her → his or her
s/he → she or he
Cf. → Compare

The authorities have reasonable grounds to believe **he's been** → **he has** been harassed, taunted, bullied, bullied, **etc.** → **et cetera.**

I.e., → **That is**, some playgrounds today are less venues for play than for harassment.

See BLUEBOOK R 1.2(e). For whether to italicize Latin phrases *see* V. CONVENTIONS: Italics.

Initialisms & Acronyms

Initialisms and acronyms are both **abbreviations**. An **acronym** is an abbreviation that can be pronounced as a word (NAFTA, NASA, OPEC, FOIA); an **initialism** is one pronounced by sounding out the letters (YMCA, EPA, FDA, AARP).

National governments **(a)** As entities, spell out. **(b)** As adjectives, abbreviate. *See* BLUEBOOK R 6.1(b), T.11(foreign & domestic countries, regions, provinces, states, cities, territories).	**(a)** • United States • United Kingdom **(b)** • U.S. delegation • U.K. practice
National & international federations as entities may be abbreviated. Do not use periods.	• United Nations → UN • UN Security Counsel • European Union → EU • EU Court of Justice
Abbreviations ending in lower-case letters: Use periods.	• a.m.
abbreviations for national governments used as adjectives, for academic or professional degrees, and any other abbreviation not commonly referred to by its initials, including states, use periods. *See* BLUEBOOK R. 6.1(b)	• U.S. policy • J.D., LL.M., Ph.D., M.D., M.B.A., M.D. • N.Y.
Abbreviations of two letters recognizable by their initials alone: do not use periods. **Abbreviations of three letters or more:** do not use periods.	• UN (*But see* examples in BLUEBOOK R. 21.7.3, using periods.) • EU, EC (*See* examples in BLUEBOOK R. 21.8.2), LA • HIV–AIDS, or HIV/AIDS (*see* II. PUNCTUATION: Slash, above.) • FCC • OSHA regulations
Plurals of abbreviations Add **s** — no apostrophe .	• NGOs • SSRIs
Abbreviation of case names in text For lengthy case names to which frequent reference may be made, a short form may be used if used consistently. *See* BLUEBOOK R 10.2.1	• Report of the Appellate Body, *United States — Import Prohibition of Certain Shrimp and Shrimp Products (**U.S. Shrimp–Turtle**)*. • *Hamdi v. Rumsfeld (**Hamdi III**)*.

Introducing abbreviations

(a) For all but the most common (and universally recognizable) abbreviations, put the short form in parentheses after the full term when it is first introduced. Do not include an article in the parentheses. Do not enclose the abbreviation in quotation marks in addition to the parentheses.

Cf. quotation marks for introducing terms of art directly into the text. *See* II. PUNCTUATION: Quotation Marks as Signals.

(b) If a common (and thus recognizable) abbreviation is used shortly after the complete name of the entity has been used, no parenthetical introduction is necessary.

(c) Conversely, an abbreviation can be spelled out in parentheses when first introduced.

(d) The main title (without the subtitle) is not considered an abbreviation and need not be introduced in parentheses.

(a) In 2002, … the Pharmaceutical Research and Manufacturers of America (**PhRMA**), a trade organization representing the innovative pharmaceutical industry, adopted the *Principles on Conduct of Clinical Trials and Communication of Clinical Trial Results* (***PhRMA Principles***).[1]

(b) In the **European Union**, privacy policy is similarly a question of interpretation among member states. **EU** policy may emanate from a central source, but how to implement that policy differs from one state to the next.

(c) In 2002, **PhRMA (Pharmaceutical Research and Manufacturers of America**), a trade organization representing the innovative pharmaceutical industry …

(d) These scenarios were presented to a panel of scientists, legal experts, journalists, and community leaders in a recent PBS television program entitled *Genes on Trial: Genetics, Behavior, and the Law.…*

… The remainder of part I summarizes ***Genes on Trial*** and introduces the issues raised by it.[2]

Articles & acronyms or initialisms

(a) **Acronyms** are treated as proper nouns and take no article.

(b) **Initialisms** ordinarily *do* take an article. If an initialism takes an article in its unabbreviated form, it should take one in its abbreviated form.

(a) A scientist at **NASA** who alleged that government editors had redacted his reports about global warming has left the agency.

(b) The scientist at **the Environmental Protection Agency** who alleged that government editors had redacted his reports about global warming has left the agency.

(b) The scientist at **the EPA** who alleged that government editors …

(c) A noun that does not take an article in its unabbreviated form (as when it is a noncountable noun) does not take one as an abbreviation, either. *(For whether and which articles to use with countable and noncountable nouns,* see Grammar Charts: Which Article? Chart.*)*

(c) The pituitary gland produces antidiuretic hormone (ADH). The production of **ADH** can be suppressed by alcohol.

---

a or **an**? Like any other noun taking an indefinite article, whether *a* or *an* is used depends on whether the initial sound of the noun is pronounced as a consonant or as a vowel.

Vowel sounds take *an*, consonant sounds take *a*.

(Consonants that are pronounced with initial vowel sounds: F, H, L, M, N, R, S, X)

Acronyms & initializations used as adjectives take an article (or not), depending on whether the noun modified takes one.

- the NAACP brief, an NAACP brief, NAACP membership has risen
- the FDA analysis, an FDA analysis, FDA records have shown
- an FOIA exemption
- a YMCA spokesperson, the YMCA spokesperson, YMCA spokespersons admitted …

Numbers (the figure or spelled out) & Numerals (the figure)

See Bluebook R 6.2 (a), (b)

In text

(a) Spell out any number beginning a sentence.

(b) Spell out 1–99 (numerals & ordinals).

(c) Spell out centuries.

(d) Use numerals in direct quotes when the original does (unless the quote *begins* with a number, then bracket the change).

(a) **Thirteen** is about the age at which children become aliens.

(b) Sterilizing the "feeble-minded" was once legal in **twenty-four** states.

(c) nineteenth century
twenty-first century

(d) "By 1930, **24** states had enacted laws to sterilize the 'feeble-minded'.…"[3]

"[**Twenty-four**] states had enacted laws to sterilize the 'feeble-minded'" by the third decade of the twentieth century.

(e) Ordinals (first, second, third) are ordinarily spelled out in text. When they are not, use 2nd, 3rd (not 2d, 3d as used in citations). No superscript.

BLUEBOOK R 6.2(b)

(e)
- By the **third** decade of the twentieth century, sterilizing the "feeble-minded" was legal in twenty-four states.
- the 102nd Congress; the 103rd Congress

(a) Fractions
Spell out & hyphenate (unless unwieldy, as when combined with a whole number).

(b) Percentages, rates, ratios, scores
(i) Spell out percentages and ratios (both the numeral and the category) (ii) unless several of these occur in the same passage.

(c) The same rule governs use of other symbols — designating measurement or monetary denomination, for example: spell out both numeral and symbol unless several appear in the same passage.

(a) Three-quarters of a million people were affected.

Cf. The cages are no larger than **eight and one-half by nine and one-quarter inches.** → 8.5" by 9.25".

(b)(i)
- About **ten percent** of the arguments are delegated.
- The odds of her winning were **three to one.**

(ii)
- The odds of their winning the lottery increased from **60,000:1** to **30,000:1** to **3,000:1.**
- The likelihood of their losing the three lotteries was **36%, 55%,** and **72%,** respectively.
- Judges use a **71-point** scale of risk assessment employing these factors to aid in sentencing. A **score of 35** or less means the defendant is eligible for house arrest or probation. If a defendant receives a **score of 35** or more, the recommendation is jail time.[4]

Numerals & parts, sections
Do not spell out the numeral when the text refers to parts or subparts of statutes or outlines or the article itself.

- **Under section 5** of the Act, the agency has extensive powers.
- See part **III** *infra* for a discussion of this policy's repercussions.

Round numbers (those ending in 0) **above one hundred** may, but need not be spelled out.

- **110; 400; 3000; 10,000**
- The crowd was estimated to number between **nine hundred** and **one thousand.**

Decimals

(a) Don't spell out.

(b) If less than 1, place a 0 in front of the decimal point.

(a) For example, in fiscal year 2004, the Department of Defense spent **$47.2** million to process FOIA requests[] and collected $537,000 in fees (**1.1%** of expenditures)....[5]

(b) A test that is no better than chance would have an ROC of **0.50**; the VRAG's ROC was **0.76**, which means that "if an offender were drawn randomly from each of the recidivist and nonrecidivist groups, there was a probability of **0.76** that the recidivist had the higher score on the VRAG."[6]

Punctuating numbers

(a) Use commas for numerals greater than 9999.

(b)(i) Numbers introducing items in a list are set out as a block are followed by a period.

(a)

9974 widgets

10,001 widgets

(b)(i) Potential recent examples of candidates for the label of "odious debts" identified by Kremer and Jayachandran include debts incurred in the following countries by [former] regimes ... :

1. Nicaragua (Anastasio Somoza reportedly looted $100–$500 million.)
2. Philippines (Ferdinand Marcos amassed a $10 billion fortune.)
3. Haiti (Duvalier regime was reported to have absconded with $900 million.)
4. South Africa (Apartheid government spent heavily on police and military to repress majority population.)
5. Congo (former Zaire) (Mobutu Sese Seko had personal accounts for $14 billion.)
6. Nigeria (Abacha reportedly held $2 billion in Swiss bank accounts in 1999.)

...[7]

(b)(ii) When the list is integrated into the text, the numbers should be enclosed in parentheses to make the separation from the framing sentence more visible. **Do not use periods**. *See also* V. CONVENTIONS: Lists.

(b)(ii) Potential recent examples of candidates for the label of "odious debts" identified by Kremer and Jayachandran include debts incurred [by former regimes] in the following countries ... : (1) Nicaragua, (2) the Philippines, (3) Haiti, (4) South Africa, (5) Congo—former Zaire, (6) Nigeria, (7) Croatia.

Dates

American style: September 11, 2001 (not 11 September 2001)

Ordinals: no superscript: September 11th 2001

Sole exception for using slashes in dates: momentous dates known as such, e.g., 9/11

Span of years

- In text: spell out. Use *through*, not *to*.
- In titles: use en dash.
- In both: do not treat like page spans; use all four digits for both years.

text: from 1997 through 2001

titles: 1997–2001

Plural of years: add **s** (no apostrophe).

Public disclosure was less likely in the 1950s and '60s.

Symbols: % $ ¶ § € &

Bluebook R 6.2 (c), (d)

In text (including footnote text)

(a) Spell out any symbol beginning a sentence. Spell out *section* or *paragraph* except, optionally, for these symbols used in federal statutes or regulations. *See* Bluebook R. 12.9, 14.10.

Insert space between symbol and number.

(b) For when to use numerals (the figure) and when to spell out a number), see V. CONVENTIONS: Numbers & Numerals, above.

(i) Use the dollar symbol **($)** with numerals (no space between **$** and the numeral). Spell out the name of the currency when the number is spelled out. Treat euros and other currencies similarly. Decimals are not spelled out.

(a) **Section 7** of the [Endangered Species Act] prescribes the steps that federal agencies must take to ensure that their actions do not jeopardize endangered wildlife and flora.... Once the consultation process contemplated by **§ 7(a)(2)** has been completed, the Secretary is required to give the agency a written biological opinion....[8]

(a) This section, which explains the applicability of **section 7**, implicitly covers [f]ederal activities within the territorial jurisdiction of the United States and upon the high seas as a result of the definition of "action" in **§ 402.02**.[9]

(b)(i)

- **three dollars and fifty cents**, **$3.50**, **$5** million
- The military squandered **$5.2** million on commodes.

(ii) Likewise, use the percent symbol **(%)** with numerals. Spell out percent when the number is spelled out. (No space between % and numeral.) Decimals are not spelled out.

(b)(ii)
- **Eighty percent** of the participants were omnivores.
- The program is funded by a flat **2.9%** tax.

(iii) When several percentages or currency figures appear in the same passage, use symbols (and numerals).

(b)(iii)
- The remaining participants were vegans, **4%**, lacto-ovos, **6%**, and vegetarians, **10%**.
- Verizon claims to have invested **$15** billion in building its FiOS service. AT&T claims to have spent **$5** to **$6** billion on its Project Lightspeed fiber-optic network.[10]

(c) Spell out section symbols **(§)** in text (except for U.S. Code (BLUE-BOOK R 12.9) or federal regulations (BLUEBOOK R 14.10). Use § symbol in all citations. Leave one space between § symbol and numeral.

(c)
- The charts in **section III** of this paper displays data from reliable sources.
- According to **§ 328.3(a)**, "waters of the United States" includes "all waters … subject to the ebb and flow of the tide." 33 C.F.R. § 328.3(a)(1) (2006).

(d) Avoid measurement symbols unless spelling out the numerals is unwieldy (as because they are decimals or fractions or because they are numerous).

(d) The cages are no larger than **8.5"** by **9.25"**.

(e) In text, ampersand(s) **(&)** are permitted only for firm names. For this use, no serial comma precedes the ampersand.

(e) The plaintiff was represented by Dewey, Cheatem & Howe.

Capitalization

Bʟᴜᴇʙᴏᴏᴋ R 8

Capitalize the first letter of the first word in a sentence (and, of course, proper nouns). For whether to capitalize the first letter of an independent clause following a colon, see II. PUNCTUATION: Colons — Colons & Capitalization.

Titles
Capitalize all words in a heading or title, including the first word of the title or subtitle (after the colon)

except

any preposition, conjunction, or article of **four letters or fewer** (unless one of these is the first word of the title or subtitle).
Bʟᴜᴇʙᴏᴏᴋ R 8(a)

Forestalling Financial Failure: The Boundaries Parents Draw Between Their Children and Their Bank Accounts

Compound words in titles
Capitalize all words in a compound, but not if the first element is only a prefix.

If the original article title does not follow this rule, in the interests of treating likes alike, modify it to do so.
But see exception for foreign titles, below.

Compounds:
Insurance-Enhanced Market Power

Cf.
The Demise of Anti-immigrant Policies

Foreign titles
In citations or in text, capitalize as these appear in the original, Bʟᴜᴇʙᴏᴏᴋ R. 20.2.(b), UNLESS these are in all caps. Then use "sentence style" capitalization, capitalizing only the first words of the title and subtitle (following the colon) and proper nouns. *See* Cʜɪᴄᴀɢᴏ Mᴀɴ-ᴜᴀʟ 17.64.

Translated foreign titles should follow *Bluebook* title conventions described above (all words except articles, conjunctions, or prepositions of fewer than five letters).

Original (speech) title in all caps, converted to sentence capitalization →
Fidel Castro Ruz, Clausura del dialogo juvenil y estudiantil de America Latina y el Caribe sobre la deuda externa, celebrado en el Palacio de las Convenciones, el 14 de Septiembre de 1985, "Año del Tercer Congreso," La Habana, Cuba (Sept. 14, 1985)

translated as "Castro Comments on Latin American Debt, Sept. 15, 1985"

Acronyms (pronounced as a word) **&** **initialisms** (pronounced as its letters): Capitalize.	• NASA, NATO, OPEC • the EPA, the FDA
Exception: Very familiar acronyms are sometimes treated as proper nouns.	*Exception:* Stocks plunged on **Nasdaq**, but not on the Dow.
Text Do not capitalize author's reference to *this article*, *part*, or *section*, etc. *Exception:* Only when article parts or sections are specifically labeled as such, as in a table of contents, are these capitalized in textual references, as well. *See* BLUEBOOK R 3.5.	This ~~Article~~ → **article** represents the industry's perspective on these issues. This **section** addresses the difficulty of applying the rule described above in **section II** to all cohorts in the sample population.

Governmental Nouns

Generally, do not capitalize if these nouns are used as adjectives unless the noun they modify is also capitalized. *See* BLUEBOOK R 8.

state Capitalize only if in a title (as of a state as a party) or if word it modifies is capitalized.	• the state of North Carolina, the appeal of Bluebeard against the State of North Carolina, the State initiated proceedings against Bluebeard, the state supreme court, the State Commissioner of Affairs
federal Capitalize only if the word it modifies is capitalized.	• U.S. federal law, federal tax policy, the Federal Reserve
Constitution Capitalize if U.S. or if part of the formal title of a constitution. **constitutional:** lower case	• the Constitution • the Constitution of North Carolina, North Carolina's constitution • constitutional provisions
Constitutional Articles, Sections, and Clauses Capitalize.	• The executive powers are designated in Article II. • That the Vice President is a creature of the executive branch is implied, if not explicit, in Section 1 of Article II. • the Fourteenth Amendment • the Commerce Clause

Framers Capitalize.	Some believe that the Constitution should be interpreted strictly according to the Framers' intent.
Acts, regulations, treaties Capitalize short forms if preceded by their full titles. Do not capitalize *section* unless it begins a sentence.	• the Endangered Species Act, the Act • the Internal Revenue Code, the Code • found in section 19 of the Animal Welfare Act
Departments or branches of government Use lower case.	• the legislative branch • the judicial branch, the judiciary • the executive branch, the executive department, the executive • The executive branch is theoretically the equal of either the legislative or the judicial branch.
Governmental offices & officials Capitalize the name of an office and capitalize the office as a title when followed by the official's name. Once the full title has been introduced, the short form is also capitalized. When a title's use is descriptive rather than formal, use lower case. *See* CHICAGO MANUAL §8.23.	• Speaker, the Speaker of the House • Speaker of the House Pelosi, Speaker Pelosi • then-senator Lyndon B. Johnson • *Cf.* former presidents Carter and Clinton
The President Capitalize, even when plural. Do not capitalize if used as an adjective: **presidential** **The chief executive** Do not capitalize (because, like the "executive branch," this is not an official title or office).	• Ladies and Gentlemen, the President of the United States— • The President runs for re-election only once. • all former Presidents of the Republic • Everyone noted that on this occasion President Bush looked surprisingly presidential; at other times the President did not. • the President is the nation's chief executive • the executive office of the President
The Administration Capitalize when preceded by the name of a President **or as short form** if it clearly refers to that President's administration.	• Bush Administration policy • this Administration's policy on the detainees • the Roosevelt Administration • numerous presidential administrations

The **cabinet & executive offices** Capitalize as designating an office or a current or past title.	• In 1977, Secretary of Defense Donald Rumsfeld was chief of staff to President Gerald Ford, and Vice President Richard Cheney was his deputy. • the former Secretary of the Interior Gail Norton • The Secretary of Homeland Security is a member of the President's cabinet.
Executive agencies, administrators **(a)** Capitalize the official title or official name of an agency or office. **(b)** Capitalize short forms only when part of the official title or name and when reference is to a particular agency or administrator previously identified. **(c)** Do not capitalize title if used generically or descriptively. **(d)** Do not capitalize plurals.	**(a)** The Department of Homeland Security, **(b)** the Department **(a)** The Environmental Protection Agency, **(b)** the Agency **(a)** Deputy Administrator for the Transportation Security Administration; **(b)** the Deputy Administrator **(a)** SEC Chairman Arthur Levitt, **(b)** the Chairman **(c)** a former commissioner of the Federal Trade Commission and later its chairman **(c)** the prison administrator **(c)**, **(d)** administrators of executive agencies **(c)**, **(d)** federal agencies
Legislative bodies & offices • Capitalize the name of an office or body or the title of a person. • Capitalize a short form only if it is a part of the official name and reference is to a particular individual previously identified. • Do not capitalize for generic reference to the person in that office.	• Congress, congressional • the House, the House of Representatives • Representative Price, Congressman Price, the representative from North Carolina, a congressman from North Carolina • the Senate, Senator Obama, the junior senator from Illinois • the U.S. Senate Committee on the Judiciary, the Judiciary Committee, the Committee • It is her ambition to be a senator.
Judicial bodies & offices Capitalize the name of an office or body or the title of a person. *Cf.* Capitalize a short form only if it is a part of the official name.	• the Supreme Court, the Court • the Chief Justice, Chief Justice Roberts • It must feel odd for Justice Ginsburg, being the only female Justice remaining on the bench. *Cf.* • It must feel odd for Justice Ginsburg to be the only female judge remaining on the bench.

Appellate courts Capitalize the formal name of a court. Capitalize "court" as a short form only for the U.S. Supreme Court. Capitalize other short forms of any appellate court.	• The Court of Appeals for the District of Columbia, the D.C. Court of Appeals, the court of appeals • The Supreme Court of North Carolina, the N.C. Supreme Court, the state supreme court • The North Carolina Court of Appeals, the Court of Appeals, the appellate court
Lower courts Capitalize formal names of courts.	• The District Court for the District of Columbia, the district court
International offices See WEBSTER's. For others, capitalize and punctuate as does that international organization.	• Secretary-General of the UN

Capitalizing Other Words

Proper nouns — the names of persons, places, things — are capitalized. Adjectives derived from proper nouns are capitalized when the origin is a person's name (Bayes, Bayesian probability; Proust, Proustian depth, Aristotle, Aristotelian logic). Adjectives derived from other sources are not capitalized when they are used less to invoke the origin than to specify or modify something else. E.g., platonic love, epicurean tastes, roman numerals. *See* CHICAGO MANUAL 8.64–8.65.

Using all caps is not permissible for emphasis; italics or another emphatic technique (such as repetition) is preferable.

Internet is usually capitalized unless a private internet is meant.	But from a subscribers' perspective, the private internets and the public [I]nternet will arguably be indistinguishable.[8]
Geographic or cultural regions may be capitalized as nouns, but not as adjectives.	• the West, western powers • the Continent, continental Europe
Historical events are capitalized.	the First World War, World War I
Abstractions should not be capitalized unless intended ironically, as if, e.g., to mock its personification.	The capitalist heart is driven by Greed alone. → The capitalist heart is driven by greed and greed alone.
Mid-sentence capitals: When a statement or question is formally introduced, it is initiated with a capital letter, regardless of the intervening punctuation.	• He wondered this aloud: Should we not intercede? • He wondered aloud, Should we not intercede? • He wondered aloud — Should we not intercede? • He spoke his thoughts aloud — We should intercede.

Cf. When the statement or question is run syntactically into the introducing words, no capital.	***Cf.*** • He wondered aloud whether we should not intercede. • He said that we should intercede.

Italics

BLUEBOOK R 7

Do not italicize common Latin phrases. Check WEBSTER'S: if the term is included, it's common enough.	ab initio ad hoc amicus curiae certiorari corpus juris de facto de jure en banc et al.	et cetera ex sequitur ex ante ex post habeas corpus inter alia mens rea modus operandi non obstante verdicto	obiter dictum per se prima facie qua quid pro quo res judicata status quo ultra vires voir dire

Italicize **(a)** foreign words or expressions (except those in WEBSTER'S), including uncommon Latin ones; **(b)** common Latin expressions **if** one or more words can be read as English; **(c)** case names in text (footnote text, too); **(d)** short form case names in text or footnotes (text or citation); and **(e)** terms introduced in text that will be components in tables or graphs. Terms of art *may* be introduced in italics, although quotation marks are preferable so as to avoid a miscue for emphasis.	**(a)** • *lex mercatoria, ipso jure* • *pari passu* clause • vin ordinaire, par excellence, communiqué ***but*** vis-à-vis, tête-à-tête (WEBSTER'S XI) **(b)** *respondeat superior* **(c)** The corporation claimed in *In re Enron Corp. Securities, Derivative & ERISA Litigation*, 235 F. Supp. 2d 549, 586–89 (S.D. Tex. 2002), that its lawyers should not be liable for corporate accountants' errors. **(d)** The corporation claimed in *Enron* that its lawyers should not be liable for corporate accountants' errors.
For italicized words or phrases within italicized phrases, use roman typeface.	Gary Myers, *Trademark Parody: Lessons from the Copyright Decision in* Campbell v. Acuff-Rose Music, Inc., 59 LAW & CONTEMP. PROBS. 181 (Spring 1996).
Italicize letters used in hypotheticals.	Let X equal the number of attorneys practicing without a license; let Y equal …

Italics for emphasis are acceptable if not overused. *See also* II. PUNCTUATION: Quotation Marks — Quotation Marks as Signals (Style: "scare quotes").

Italics & plurals or possessives: Do not italicize the **s** for a plural of an italicized term or the **'s** for a possessive.	• The table sagged under unread *New Yorker***s**. • The *New Yorker***'s** articles are always of interest (if one has the time to read them).

Lists

See CHICAGO MANUAL 6.124–6.129

Lists run into text: Use numerals in parentheses (no period) or, when a subset of the numerals, letters (in parentheses, no period).

If list is introduced with an independent clause, follow that sentence with a colon; if it is introduced by only a phrase, no punctuation should precede the list.

Punctuate the end of each item in the list with a comma (unless one or more items have internal commas, then use semicolons); connect last two with *and* or *or*.

(1) Numbers are best, followed by **(a)** letters when a subset of numbers is needed, but **(b)** no bullets.

List in text:
Such routines have the advantages of providing[] (1) parameter estimates that are constrained to be mathematically reasonable values by, for example, requiring each variance component to be between zero and one; (2) significance tests of each parameter; and[] (3) goodness-of-fit indices to evaluate the adequacy of the genetic model.[12]

Lists set out from text as block

Mark each item with numerals followed by a period. (Parentheses to clarify separation of the numeral from the surrounding text are unnecessary.)

Such lists are preferably introduced with a complete sentence followed by a colon.

1. numbers best,
   a. letters when subset of numbers, and
   b. no bullets

List set out from text:
These countries are candidates for the label of "odious debts" incurred by former regimes:
   1. Nicaragua
   2. Philippines
   3. Haiti
   4. South Africa
   5. Former Zaire, now Congo
   6. Nigeria
   7. Croatia[13]

Punctuation of items in a block list:

If the list is introduced with an independent clause and a colon, do not punctuate end of each item unless it is a complete sentence.

Capitalize the initial letter of each item.

Cf.

When introduced with an independent clause and a colon, **items stated as sentences** should all have the same terminal punctuation — periods, semicolons, or commas (except the last, which should always be followed by a period).

Use terminal commas or semicolons for all but the last item if the last two items are linked with a conjunction.

Capitalize the initial letter of each item.

If the list is introduced with a phrase and the list completes the sentence the phrase begins, end each item with a comma (or a semicolon, if any one item has internal commas), just as a list run into text would be punctuated. End with a period.

Items are not capitalized unless they are proper nouns.

Such routines have the advantages of providing the following:

1. Parameter estimates
2. Significance tests
3. Goodness-of-fit indices[14]

Cf.

These former regimes subjected their countries to debts now considered odious:

1. Anastasio Somoza (Nicaragua) reportedly looted $100–$500 million.
2. Ferdinand Marcos (Philippines) amassed a $10 billion fortune.
3. The Duvalier regime (Haiti) was reported to have absconded with $900 million.
4. The Apartheid government (South Africa) spent heavily on police and military to repress majority population.
5. Mobutu Sese Seko (Congo, formerly Zaire) had personal accounts for $14 billion.
6. Abacha (Nigeria) reportedly held $2 billion in Swiss bank accounts in 1999.
7. Tudjman (Croatia) looted unknown amounts, suppressed media, and violently attacked his political opponents.[15]

Such routines have the advantages of providing

1. parameter estimates that are constrained to be mathematically reasonable values by, for example, requiring each variance component to be between zero and one;
2. significance tests of each parameter; and
3. goodness-of-fit indices to evaluate the adequacy of the genetic model.[16]

Bullets, although popular and useful in other contexts, are informal and inappropriate for the formal style of most law journals and legal documents.

Charts & Tables

Charts and tables are divided by lines and arranged in formats that make punctuation for the sake of the separation and interrelationship of their components unnecessary, particularly when the components are expressed as words or phrases, capitalized (title style). When the components are in sentence-style, however, normal textual punctuation rules apply: no need for terminal periods unless the components are stated as independent clauses.

Spelling Conventions

WEBSTER'S XI

Unconventional spelling: Correct but non-U.S. spelling of words in **direct quotes** should be left alone (*see* III. QUOTATIONS: Insertions & Omissions — Unconventional material in quotation). But spelling in U.S. publications or documents should be made to conform with U.S. spelling conventions.

behaviour → behavior
analyse → analyze
whilst → while (or although, whereas)
  See IV. USAGE & STYLE (while / although / whereas), above.

Spelling & hyphenation
For whether words are hyphenated or closed up, see WEBSTER'S. If the word is not included, treat it according to these guidelines:

1. The tendency of the language is to move from open compounds to closed (policy making body → policy-making body → policymaking body) (CHICAGO MANUAL 7.84, 7.90);
2. The logic of treating like words alike (policymaking → decisionmaking);
3. Consistent treatment of the same word.

- policyholder (WEBSTER'S), policymaking
- decisionmaking, decisionmaking body (NB: CHICAGO MANUAL § 7.90 treats this noun as two separate words. It hyphenates the adjective, as does BLACK'S. The choice is the editor's call, but one that should be made consistently.)

Prefixes, Suffixes, & Hyphens

See Chicago Manual §7.90

Prefixes, suffixes, & hyphens (check the **dictionary**)

(a) General rule: hyphens are used with *all-, ex-, quasi-, self-, -elect.*

(a)
- all-encompassing
- ex-president
- quasi-public
- self-assessment
- mayor-elect

(b) Use a hyphen between prefixes and single capitalized words or numerals.

(b) non-American, post-9/11

(c) Hyphenate the prefix when it precedes a hyphenated compound.

(c)
- non-tennis-playing members
- non-self-executing orders

But

Use an **en dash** (rather than a hyphen) between any prefix and a non-hyphenated (open) compound of two or more words.

en dash
- pre–Civil War
- non–Paris Club claimants
- non–Article III courts
- non–social scientist

(d) Use a hyphen to avoid ambiguity.

(d) re-formation of river ice

Prefixes, suffixes, and hyphens

These prefixes are generally consistently closed
unless
- they precede a capitalized word or a number (including a number spelled out);
or
- they precede an open (unhyphenated) compound — then use an en-dash (non–arm's length) *see* II. PUNCTUATION: En Dash — En Dashes and Words, above;
or

ante → antedate

anti → anticoagulant, *but* anti-ideological, anti-inflammatory, anti-American

bi → bimodal

bio → biochemical

co → cosponsor, coauthors, *but* co-own, co-opt, co-officiate

counter → counterinsurgency

cyber → cyberpunk

extra → extraordinary

hyper → hyperlink

hypo → hypotension

- they precede a closed (hyphenated) compound — then use a hyphen (non-civil-rights cases);

or

- running the syllables together causes the repetition of the same vowel sound (anti-ideological, co-ownership, mega-analysis;

or

- they might be misread (antiimigration → anti-immigration; coworker → co-worker; coopt → co-opt, *but*, exceptionally, cooperate; nonodious → non-odious).

See Chicago Manual 7.90(3).

inter → interrelate

intra → intramuscular, *but* intra-arterial

macro → macrostructure

mega → megacorporation

meta → metadiscourse, *but* meta-analysis

micro → microeconomics

mid → midway, *but* mid-fifteenth century, mid-teens

mini → minipark

multi → multiracial

neo → neoconservative

non → nongovernmental, nonelected, *but* non-European, non–arm's length, non-self-executing, non-civil-rights cases

over → overrate, overinvest

post → postindustrial, postmodern, *but* post-Victorian, post-nineteenth century, post-trial

pre → preexist, *but* pre-engineered, pre-9/11, pre-Jurassic

pro → proactive, proabortion, *but* pro-social, pro-family

proto → prototype

pseudo → pseudoscience

psycho → psycholinguistics

re → reeducate, reelect; *but* re-do, re-election

semi → semiliterate, semierect

socio → sociopolitical

sub → subtitle, suboptimal

super → superadd, superfan

supra → supraliminal

trans → translocation, transatlantic, transpacific

ultra → ultraliberal

un → unsung, unnerved, unnoticeable

under → underutilize

URLs

<small>Bluebook</small> R 18.2

Signal title (date) (on file with *Law & Contemp. Probs.*), *available at* http://www…. (last visited Mar. 21, 2005) (explanatory parenthetical).

If website is dated, omit (last visited) parenthetical. *See* <small>Bluebook</small> R 18.2.3(e), (f).

See, e.g., Press Release, Trans Atl. Consumer Dialogue, U.S.–EU Summit Puts Business CEOs Ahead of Consumer Groups (June 23, 2004) (on file with *Law & Contemp. Probs.*) *available at* http://www.tacd.org/press/?id=39 (last visited Mar. 21, 2005) (announcing a boycott of a summit of the Transatlantic Economic Partnership by TACD when business groups were offered a meeting with Presidents of the United States and the European Council, but consumer groups were denied a similar meeting).

Interviews

Nonconfidential interviews should be cited as advised in Bluebook R. 7.1.4.

Confidential interviews, on the other hand, pose the obvious problem of the editor's inability to vouch for the veracity of the material. When the text of the interview is provided (and often it is not), the substance of the conversation can be confirmed. When, however, neither a transcript nor the interviewer's notes are available, and the person interviewed is likewise unknown or otherwise unavailable, the substance of the discussion reported by the author cannot be verified.

Ideally, the author will trust the editor with a confidential copy of the interview transcript or of her notes, redacted as necessary. But — understandably — some authors are not comfortable with this practice. In such cases, a disclaimer is a reasonable way to signal the editor's inability to verify the accuracy of the author's account. The author should not take umbrage at this practice; it implies nothing about the author's trustworthiness; rather, it indicates to the reader simply that the account cannot be independently verified.

Absent notes or a transcript, one approach to verifying the information in a confidential interview is to ask the author the kinds of questions newspaper editors ask their reporters: "How well do you know your source? What [if any] ax [might he be] grinding? Why is he insisting on anonymity? Has he been reliable in the past? Do you believe what he says? Is there any corroborating information?" [17]

Absent such cross-examination (which might well be more offensive than the disclaimer itself), a disclaimer could be phrased to indicate the source of the impediment, like this:

> "Because the Human Science Foundation's Human Subject rules were implicated by the author's confidential interviews, the editors of *Law & Contemporary Problems* was unable to independently verify the content of those interactions." [18]

Or, if the reason is the author's assurance of confidentiality, "Because of the promises of confidentiality involved in this interview, *Law & Contemporary Problems* is unable to independently verify its content."

Nonetheless, editors should be aware that permitting authors to publish results based on confidential sources is risky business,[19] and the better practice is to insist that the author supply at least the text or contemporaneous notes of the interview. Remember, though: Ultimately the law review retains the discretion to reject articles that depend on sources that cannot be independently verified.

Sample Law Journal Outline Conventions

I

INTRODUCTION

II

HEADING TWO

A. Subheading One [Capitalize]

Skip one line before beginning text.

1. Subdivision One [Capitalize]
Text begins on the next line.

2. Further Subdivisions Should Be Avoided.
   But if, in rare instances, they cannot be, follow this form:

a. Subdivision level two. Text continues on same line as subheading. Only the first word and proper nouns are capitalized. The subheading is italicized and followed by a period to keep it distinct from the text.

   (1) Subdivision level three. Text continues on same line as subheading, etc.

      (a) Subdivision level four. Text continues on same line as subheading, etc.

         (i) Subdivision level five. Text continues on same line as subheading, etc.

B. Subheading Two

Skip one line before beginning text.

Paragraph Headings

1. Paragraph Heading One. Ordinarily, a paragraph heading should be used when more than one paragraph heading is called for and when each heading stands for a single paragraph. Material more lengthy or developed than a single paragraph should follow the outline format above.

2. Paragraph Heading Two.

If, however, the enumerated items include more than one paragraph, the text should begin on the next line, indented.

Initial paragraph numbers are unnecessary but desirable; if paragraphs have subdivisions, though, initial numbers or letters are necessary.

3. Paragraph Heading Three. The style for further subdivisions—a., (1), (a), (i)—may be used when appropriate for paragraph headings. Text begins on same line as the subheading.

Endnotes

I • Grammar

1. Elizabeth Chambliss, *When Do Facts Persuade? Some Thoughts on the Market for "Empirical Legal Studies,"* 71 Law & Contemp. Probs. 17 (Spring 2008).

2. Benedict Kingsbury et al., *The Emergence of Global Administrative Law*, 68 Law & Contemp. Probs. 15, 28 (Summer/Autumn 2005).

3. Janet McLean, *Divergent Legal Conceptions of the State; Implications for Global Administrative Law*, 68 Law & Contemp. Probs. 167, 170 n.4 (Summer/Autumn 2005).

4. *Id.*

II • Punctuation

1. Benedict Kingsbury et al., *The Emergence of Global Administrative Law*, 68 Law & Contemp. Probs. 15, 21 (Summer/Autumn 2005).

2. *Id.* at 22.

3. Kalypso Nicolaidis & Gregory Shaffer, *Transnational Mutual Recognition Regimes: Governance Without Global Government*, 68 Law & Contemp. Probs. 263, 267 n.7 (Summer/Autumn 2005).

4. Walter Mattli & Tim Büthe, *Global Private Governance: Lessons from a National Model of Setting Standards in Accounting*, 68 Law & Contemp. Probs. 225, 226 (Summer/ Autumn 2005).

5. Nicolaidis & Shaffer, *supra* note 3, at 286.

6. Mattli & Büthe, *supra* note 4, at 256 n.108.

7. Nicolaidis & Shaffer, *supra* note 3, at 273 n.20.

8. *See id.* (quotation modified for illustrative purposes).

9. David Dyzenhaus, *The Rule of (Administrative) Law in International Law*, 68 Law & Contemp. Probs. 127, 129 (Summer/Autumn 2005).

10. Richard B. Stewart, *U.S. Administrative Law: A Model for Global Administrative Law?* 68 Law & Contemp. Probs. 63, 100 (Summer/Autumn 2005).

11. Kingsbury et al., *supra* note 1, at 24.

12. Scott M. Lassman, *Transparency and Innuendo: An Alternative to Reactive Over-Disclosure*, 69 LAW & CONTEMP. PROBS. 69, 81 (Summer 2006).

13. Mattli & Büthe, *supra* note 4, at 252.

14. *Id.* at 250.

15. Janet McLean, *Divergent Legal Conceptions of the State; Implications for Global Administrative Law*, 68 LAW & CONTEMP. PROBS. 167, 173 (Summer/Autumn 2005).

16. *See* Girardeau A. Spann, *Just Do It*, 67 LAW & CONTEMP. PROBS. 11, 13 (Summer 2004) ("Conservatives tend to believe that the history of discrimination has little application to current race relations because that history has been largely superseded by the gains of the civil rights movement.").

17. Ralf Michaels, *The Re-Statement of Non-State Law: The State, Choice of Law, and the Challenge from Global Legal Pluralism*, 51 WAYNE L. REV. 1209, 1238 (Fall 2005).

18. Spann, *supra* note 16, at 13.

19. *Id.*

20. Stuart Minor Benjamin, *Evaluating E-Rulemaking: Public Participation and Political Institutions*, 55 DUKE L.J. 893, 919–20 (March 2006).

21. Mattli & Büthe, *supra* note 4, at 231.

22. Erica Beecher-Monas & Edgar Garcia-Rill, *Genetic Predictions of Future Dangerousness: Is There a Blueprint for Violence?* 69 LAW & CONTEMP. PROBS. 301, 303 n.12 (Winter/Spring 2006).

23. Martin Shapiro,"*Deliberative,*" "*Independent*" *Technocracy v. Democratic Politics: Will the Globe Echo the E.U.?* 68 LAW & CONTEMP. PROBS. 341, 353 (Summer/Autumn 2005) ("The E.U.").

24. John Q. Barrett, *A Commander's Power, A Civilian's Reason: Justice Jackson's* Korematsu *Dissent*, 68 LAW & CONTEMP. PROBS. 57, 75 n.48 (Spring 2005).

25. Martin S. Flaherty, *The Future and Past of U.S. Foreign Relations Law*, 67 LAW & CONTEMP. PROBS. 169, 188 (Autumn 2004).

26. Spann, *supra* note 16, at 13.

27. Lawrence Lessig, *Foreword, Cultural Environmentalism @ 10*, 70 LAW & CONTEMP. PROBS. 1, 1 (Spring 2007).

28. H.W. FOWLER, A DICTIONARY OF MODERN ENGLISH USAGE 623 (2d ed. 1965).

29. Ralf Michaels, *Beyond the State? — Rethinking Private Law*, remarks in brochure for Joint Conference of the American Journal of Comparative Law and Rabels Zeitschrift für Ausländisches und Internationales Privatrecht, Max Planck Institute, Hamburg, July 12–14, 2007.

30. Sabino Cassese, *European Administrative Proceedings*, 68 LAW & CONTEMP. PROBS. 21, 33 (Winter 2004).

31. Beecher-Monas & Garcia-Rill, *supra* note 22, at 303 n.12.

32. *See* Cassese, *supra* note 26, at 34 (using parentheses rather than em dashes).

33. Michaels, *supra* note 17, at 1211.

34. *See* Dyzenhaus, *supra* note 9, at 129 (no enumeration in original).

35. Kingsbury et al., *supra* note 1, at 30.

36. John L. Coffee, Jr., *Understanding Enron: "It's About the Gatekeepers, Stupid,"* 57 Bus. Law. 1403, 1405 (2002).

37. Tim Büthe, *The Globalization of Health and Safety Standards: Delegation of Regulatory Authority in the SPS Agreement of the GATT 1994 (WTO) Treaty,* 71 Law & Contemp. Probs. 243 (Winter 2008) (paraphrased).

38. Barbara Koremenos, *When, What, and Why do States Choose to Delegate?,* 71 Law & Contemp. Probs. 153 (Winter 2008).

39. Michaels, *supra* note 17, at 1212.

40. Karen Rothenberg & Alice Wang, *The Scarlet Gene: Behavioral Genetics, Criminal Law, and Racial and Ethnic Stigma,* 69 Law & Contemp. Probs. 343, 347 (Winter/Spring 2006).

41. *See* Beecher-Monas & Garcia-Rill, *supra* note 22, at 301 (quotation modified for illustrative purposes).

III • Quotations

1. Brenda Sims Blackwell & Clark D. Cunningham, *Taking the Punishment out of the Process: From Substantive Criminal Justice Through Procedural Justice to Restorative Justice,* 67 Law & Contemp. Probs. 59, 71 n.70 (Autumn 2004) (quoting Kathleen Daly & Russ Immarigeon, *The Past, Present, and Future of Restorative Justice: Some Critical Reflections,* 1 Contemp. Just. Rev. 21, 37 (1998)).

2. James Salzman, *Decentralized Administrative Law in the Organization for Economic Cooperation and Development,* 68 Law & Contemp. Probs. 189, 208 (Summer/Autumn 2005) (quoting Nicholas Hildyard, *Snouts in the Trough: Export Credit Agencies, Corporate Welfare and Policy Incoherence,* ECA Watch, at http://www.eca-watch.org/eca/snouts4.html (last visited Feb. 20, 2005)).

3. *Id.*

4. Walter Mattli & Tim Büthe, *Global Private Governance: Lessons from a National Model of Setting Standards in Accounting,* 68 Law & Contemp. Probs. 225, 249 (Summer/Autumn 2005) (quoting Robert Herz, Address to the American Institute of Certified Public Accountants, (Dec. 12, 2003) (on file with authors)).

5. *Id.* at 245 (quoting Paul B. W. Miller et al., The FASB: The People, the Process, and the Politics 55–58 (4th ed. 1998)).

6. Blackwell & Cunningham, *supra* note 1, at 82 (quoting Douglas Ammar & Tosha Downey, *Transformative Criminal Defense Practice: Truth, Love and Individual Rights—the Innovative Approach of the Georgia Justice Project,* 31 Fordham Urb. L. J. 49, 55 (2003)).

7. Paul Schiff Berman, *Conflict of Laws, Globalization, and Cosmopolitan Pluralism,* 51 Wayne L. Rev. 1105, 1133–35 (Fall 2005) (citations omitted and hyphens added to compound modifiers).

8. *Id.*

IV • Usage & Style

1. Bryan A. GARNER, A DICTIONARY OF MODERN LEGAL USAGE 924 (2d ed. 1995). *See also* H. W. FOWLER, A DICTIONARY OF MODERN ENGLISH USAGE 687, (2d ed. 1965).

2. Karen Rothenburg & Alice Wang, *The Scarlet Gene: Behavioral Genetics, Criminal Law, and Racial and Ethnic Stigma*, 69 LAW & CONTEMP. PROBS. 343, 358 (Winter/Spring 2006).

3. Inscription on James Farley Post Office, New York City, paraphrasing line from Herodotus' *Histories* (8.98).

4. Luke A. Lantta, *The Post-Zelman Voucher Battleground: Where to Turn after Federal Challenges to Blaine Amendments Fail*, 67 LAW & CONTEMP. PROBS. 213, 240–41 (Summer 2004).

5. Walter Mattli & Tim Büthe, *Global Private Governance: Lessons from a National Model of Setting Standards in Accounting*, 68 LAW & CONTEMP. PROBS. 225, 254 (Summer/Autumn 2005) (using "as").

6. Tim Büthe, *The Globalization of Health and Safety Standards: Delegation of Regulatory Authority in the SPS Agreement of the GATT 1994 (WTO) Treaty*, 71 LAW & CONTEMP. PROBS 219, 239 (Winter 2008).

7. David A. Elder, *Truth, Accuracy and Neutral Reportage: Beheading the Media Jabberwock's Attempts to Circumvent* New York Times v. Sullivan, VAND. J. ENT. L. & PRAC. 551, 823 n.1687 (Spring 2007).

8. Rothenburg & Wang, *supra* note 2, at 346.

9. *Hardy v. Johns-Manville Sales Corp.*, 681 F.2d 334, 347 (5th Cir 1982).

10. Garrett Epps, *The Antebellum Political Background of the Fourteenth Amendment*, 67 LAW & CONTEMP. PROBS. 175, 194 (Summer 2004).

11. Patricia Wald, *The Rhetoric of Results and the Results of Rhetoric: Judicial Writings*, 62 U. CHI. L.R. 1371, 1382 (Fall 1995).

12. Benedict Kingsbury et al., *The Emergence of Global Administrative Law*, 68 LAW & CONTEMP. PROBS. 15, 54 (Summer/Autumn 2005) ("It applies only when …").

13. D.H. Kaye, *Behavioral Genetics Research and Criminal DNA Databases*, 69 LAW & CONTEMP. PROBS. 259, 278 (Winter/Spring 2006) ("However, whereas …").

14. Mark E. Budnitz, *The High Cost of Mandatory Consumer Arbitration*, 67 LAW & CONTEMP. PROBS. 133, 159 (Winter/Spring 2004) (using "when … when").

15. Martin S. Flaherty, *The Future and Past of U.S. Foreign Relations Law*, 67 LAW & CONTEMP. PROBS. 169, 175 (Autumn 2004).

16. Adam Winkler, *Corporate Law or the Law of Business?: Stakeholders and Corporate Governance at the End of History*, 67 LAW & CONTEMP. PROBS. 109, 130 (Autumn 2004).

17. David Dyzenhaus, *The Rule of (Administrative) Law in International Law*, 68 LAW & CONTEMP. PROBS. 127, 145 (Summer/Autumn 2005).

18. Kingsbury et al., *supra* note 12, at 24.

19. Erica Beecher-Monas & Edgar Garcia-Rill, *Genetic Predictions of Future Dangerousness: Is There a Blueprint for Violence?* 69 Law & Contemp. Probs. 301, 304 (Winter/Spring 2006) (using "Although").

20. Rothenburg & Wang, *supra* note 2, at 345 (using "While").

21. Beecher-Monas & Garcia-Rill, *supra* note 19, at 303 n.12.

22. Laura A. Baker et al., *Behavioral Genetics: The Science of Antisocial Behavior*, 69 Law & Contemp. Probs. 7, 13 (Winter/Spring 2006) (using "yet").

23. Kingsbury et al., *supra* note 12, at 27.

24. Stuart Minor Benjamin, *Evaluating E-Rulemaking: Public Participation and Political Institutions*, 55 Duke L.J. 893, 904 (March 2006).

25. Rothenburg & Wang, *supra* note 8, at 347.

26. Beecher-Monas & Garcia-Rill, *supra* note 19, at 304.

27. Dyzenhaus, *supra* note 17, at 127.

28. Rothenberg & Wang, *supra* note 8, at 363.

29. Jedediah Purdy, Being America 134 (2003).

30. Dyzenhaus, *supra* note 17, at 164.

31. Kingsbury et al., *supra* note 12, at 56.

32. Beecher-Monas & Garcia-Rill, *supra* note 19, at 330.

33. Purdy, *supra* note 29, at 127.

34. James Boyle, *A Politics of Intellectual Property: Environmentalism for the Net?* 47 Duke L.J. 87, 87 (1997).

35. Budnitz, *supra* note 14, at 154.

36. Owen D. Jones, *Behavioral Genetics and Crime*, 69 Law & Contemp. Probs. 81, 90 (Winter/Spring 2006) ("[T]here is a marked tendency in discussions of behavioral genetics and crime to focus on violent behaviors ....")

37. *See* Rothenberg & Wang, *supra* note 2, at 349 (quotation modified for illustrative purposes).

38. *Id.*

39. Purdy, *supra* note 28, at 136–37 (2003).

40. *Id.*

41. *Id.*

42. *Id.*

43. *Id.* at 142.

44. Eyal Benvenisti, *The Interplay Between Actors as a Determinant of the Evolution of Administrative Law in International Institutions*, 68 Law & Contemp. Probs. 319, 329 (Summer/Autumn 2005).

45. Ralf Michaels, *The Re-Statement of Non-State Law: The State, Choice of Law, and the Challenge from Global Legal Pluralism*, 51 Wayne L. Rev. 1209, 1217 (Fall 2005).

46. Sheila Jasanoff, *Transparency in Public Science: Purposes, Reasons, Limits*, 69 LAW & CONTEMP. PROBS. 21, 24 (Summer 2006).

47. *Id.*

48. *Id.* at 42.

49. Susan P. Crawford, *Network Rules*, 70 LAW & CONTEMP. PROBS. 51, 66 (Spring 2007).

50. Beecher-Monas & Garcia-Rill, *supra* note 19, at 306.

51. James W. Conrad Jr., *Open Secrets: The Widespread Availability of Information About the Health and Environmental Effects of Chemicals*, 69 LAW & CONTEMP. PROBS. 158–59 (Summer 2006) (citations omitted).

52. H. Jefferson Powell,*"Cardozo's Foot": The Chancellor's Conscience and Constructive Trusts*, 56 LAW & CONTEMP. PROBS. 7 (Summer 1993) (citations omitted).

53. J.B. Ruhl & James Salzman, *In Defense of Regulatory Peer Review*, 84 WASH. U. L. REV. 1, 2 (2006) (citations omitted).

54. *See* Scott M. Lassman, *Transparency and Innuendo: An Alternative to Reactive Over-Disclosure*, 69 LAW & CONTEMP. PROBS. 69, 72 (Summer 2006) (citations omitted and quotation modified for illustrative purposes).

55. *Id.*

56. *See id.* (quotation modified for illustrative purposes).

57. *See id.* (quotation modified for illustrative purposes).

V • Conventions

1. Scott M. Lassman, *Transparency and Innuendo: An Alternative to Reactive Over-Disclosure*, 69 LAW & CONTEMP. PROBS. 69–70 (Summer 2006).

2. Karen Rothenberg & Alice Wang, *The Scarlet Gene: Behavioral Genetics, Criminal Law, and Racial and Ethnic Stigma*, 69 LAW AND CONTEMP. PROBS. 343, 343–44 (Winter/Spring 2006).

3. Charles C. Mann, *Behavioral Genetics in Transition*, 264 SCIENCE 1686, 1686 (1994), *quoted in* Erica Beecher-Monas & Edgar Garcia-Rill, *Genetic Predictions of Future Dangerousness: Is There a Blueprint for Violence?* 69 LAW & CONTEMP. PROBS. 301, 304 n.15 (Winter/Spring 2006).

4. Erica Beecher-Monas & Edgar Garcia-Rill, *Genetic Predictions of Future Dangerousness: Is There a Blueprint for Violence?* 69 LAW & CONTEMP. PROBS. 301, 311 n.47 (Winter/Spring 2006).

5. Michael Russo, *Are Bloggers Representatives of the News Media Under the Freedom of Information Act?*, 40 COLUM. J.L. & SOC. PROBS. 225, 241 n.86 (Winter 2006) (citations omitted).

6. Beecher-Monas & Garcia-Rill, *supra* note 4, at 321 n.127 (quoting VERNON L. QUINSEY ET AL., VIOLENT OFFENDERS: APPRAISING AND MANAGING RISK 190 (1998).

7. James V. Feinerman, *Odious Debt, Old and New: The Legal Intellectual History of an Idea*, 71 LAW & CONTEMP. PROBS. 192, 217 (Autumn 2007) (citing Michael Kremer & Seema Jayachandran, *Odious Debt*, FIN & DEV., June 2002, at 36).

8. *National Ass'n of Home Builders v. Defenders of Wildlife*, 127 S. Ct. 2518, 2526 (2007).

9. 51 *Fed. Reg.* 19937.

10. Susan P. Crawford, *Network Rules*, 70 LAW & CONTEMP. PROBS. 51, 63 (Spring 2007).

11. *Id.* at 67.

12. Laura A. Baker et al., *Behavioral Genetics: The Science of Antisocial Behavior*, 69 LAW & CONTEMP. PROBS. 7, 12 (Winter/Spring 2006).

13. *See* Feinerman, *supra* note 7, at 217 (quotation modified for illustrative purposes).

14. *See* Baker et al, *supra* note 12, at 12 (quotation modified for illustrative purposes).

15. *See* Feinerman, *supra* note 7, at 217 (quotation modified for illustrative purposes).

16. *See* Baker et al, *supra* note 12, at 12 (quotation modified for illustrative purposes).

17. E-mail from Eric Easton, Professor of Law, Univ. of Baltimore School of Law, to Joan Magat (August 8, 2008) (on file with author).

18. Elizabeth A. Hoffman, *The "Haves" and "Have-Nots" Within the Organization*, 71 LAW & CONTEMP. PROBS. 53, 53 n.* (Spring 2008).

19. Publication of empirical legal studies based on proprietary data, for example, resulted not only in unreliable conclusions, but in fierce criticism of a publication process that would permit such material to be published at all. *See* Elizabeth Chambliss, *When Do Facts Persuade? Some Thoughts on the Market for "Empirical Legal Studies,"* 71 LAW & CONTEMP. PROBS. 17, 28–30 (Spring 2008) (recounting criticism resulting from publication of Richard H. Sander, *A Systematic Analysis of Affirmative Action in American Law Schools*, 57 STAN. L. REV. 367 (2004)). See also the admonitions of two such critics cited by Chambliss: Michele Landis Dauber, *The Big Muddy*, 57 STAN. L. REV. 1899, 1907–08 (2005) ("In my view, the Stanford Law Review should not have permitted Sander to publish his results while maintaining the secrecy of the underlying data. Access to data supporting research results is a central feature of free scientific inquiry, and even if Sander chose to disregard this principle, the editors of the Law Review should have upheld it."); Lee Epstein & Gary King, *The Rules of Inference*, 69 U. CHI. L. REV. 1, 132 (2002) ("We recommend that law reviews, at a minimum, require documentation of empirical data with as much specificity as they do for textual documentation. And, just as for textual documentation, this should be a prerequisite for publication.").

Glossary & Index

Abbreviations: short forms of words. These may be a part of the abbreviated word followed by a period (contemporary → contemp.) or two letters followed by periods (U.S., U.K.) or not (UN, EU), or three letters or more without periods. Abbreviations pronounced by sounding out the letters are **initialisms** (EPA, FDA, AARP); abbreviations pronounced as a word (NAFTA, NASA, OPEC) are **acronyms**.

Absolute Phrase: a cluster of words that modifies the whole sentence and often precedes it, 9

Acronym: an abbreviation that can be pronounced as a word (NAFTA, NASA, OPEC), 87–88

ADJECTIVES: words defining or modifying nouns

Adjective Clause: two or more words including a subject and a verb that modify a noun. (The lad**, who had but one life to give**)

Adjective Phrase: two or more words that modify a noun (The **rather small** lad**, sensing courage surge from head to knees**)

Person: narrative point of view, as expressed by the pronoun chosen: first person refers to the writer ("I," "we"), second, to the reader ("you"), and third ("he," "she," "they," or "it" — which can of course refer to the sentence's subject or the article's topic), 78–79

PHRASE: a cluster of two words or more. Clauses, which consists of a subject and a verb, are necessarily phrases, but not all phrases are clauses.
> **Participial Phrase:** a cluster of words that modify the subject in the main clause
> > *cf.* absolute phrase, 9
> > dangling participial phrase, 12

Prefixes: a syllable fused or attached with a hyphen to the beginning of a word that produce a derivative word (ex-convict; preschool)
> hyphens & spelling, 102–03

Pronouns, Relative: including "that," "which," "who"
> & commas, 32
> list of relative pronouns, 16
> & no commas, 33
> & parallel structure, 14
> & sexism, *see* xi
> "that" & verbosity, 68

Punctuation, Placement vis-à-vis footnotes, 50

Quotation Marks (" "): punctuation marks that signal a direct quotation, a term of art, or irony
> placement vis-à-vis other punctuation, 49–50
> scare quotes, 49
> with terms of art, 48

Relative Pronouns
> list of relative pronouns, 16
> unambiguous usage of "that," "which," 62, 64, 65

Rhetorical Question: a question posed by the writer to pique the reader's interest, not to prompt an answer (although, intrigued, the reader will expect the text that follows to in fact address, if not answer, the question), 76